Whaling in the
North Atlantic

From Earliest Times to the Mid-19th Century

Jean-Pierre Proulx

Studies in Archaeology
Architecture and History

National Historic Parks and Sites Branch
Parks Canada
Environment Canada

Available in Canada through authorized bookstore agents and other bookstores, or by mail from the Canadian Government Publishing Centre, Supply and Services Canada, Hull, Quebec, Canada K1A 0S9.

L'original français s'intitule *La pêche de la baleine dans l'Atlantique Nord jusqu'au milieu du XIXe siècle* (n^o de catalogue R61-2/9-30F). En vente au Canada par l'entremise de nos agents libraires agréés et autres librairies, ou par la poste au Centre d'édition du gouvernement du Canada, Approvisionnements et Services Canada, Hull, Québec, Canada K1A 0S9.

Price Canada: $6.50
Price other countries: $7.80
Price subject to change without notice.

Catalogue No.: R61-2/9-30E
ISBN: 0-660-12068-2
ISSN: 0821-1027

Published under the authority
of the Minister of the Environment,
Ottawa, 1986.

Translated by the Department of the Secretary of State.
Cover design: Louis D. Richard

The opinions expressed in this report are those of the author and not necessarily those of Environment Canada.

Parks Canada publishes the results of its research in archaeology, architecture and history. A list of titles is available from Research Publications, Parks Canada, 1600 Liverpool Court, Ottawa, Ontario K1A 1G2

CONTENTS

Submitted for publication 1982 by Jean-Pierre Proulx, Parks Canada, Ottawa.

INTRODUCTION

Our planet is called Earth, yet 70.8 per cent of its surface area is covered with water. All life forms on the planet require water, and in one way or another all this water comes from the sea. The sea is the cradle and the motor of life. In many ways it constitutes a more habitable environment than the land: it is less subject to changes and extremes of temperature, it offsets gravity better, it is more uniform, and it contains everything essential for life. There is an unimaginable variety of life forms in the sea, ranging from microscopic animals to blue whales that weigh 150 tons (three times the weight of the biggest dinosaur and 36 times the weight of an adult elephant). Larger species feed on smaller ones, and at the top of the pyramid are the great whales, which must eat the equivalent of 400 billion diatoms just to survive for a few hours.

Humanity, though at the top of the hierarchy of living things, is still largely ignorant of the ocean world. Until very recently we knew less about it than about the bright side of the moon, yet in a few years our survival may depend on the food resources of the ocean. In 1961 President John F. Kennedy said that the sea was not a curiosity but a necessity.[1] Our ignorance gives rise to a wasteful, destructive and inefficient exploitation of those resources. Even today we get only slightly over one per cent of our food from the sea.[2] Yet people have been fishing for thousands of years. The long delay in making better use of marine resources had a great variety of causes, the most general and important probably being that fishing required people to leave their natural habitat, the land, and venture out into the watery world beyond. This required the development of appropriate techniques based on an empirical knowledge of the seas — knowledge that took centuries to acquire. Generally speaking, the extent of knowledge of ocean life depended on the size of the animal: the larger the animal, the less well known it was because there were no effective methods for capturing it. The great whales are a good example of this. Only in modern times, and more particularly in this century, with several nations engaged in intensive hunting, has science been able to acquire useful data on these mammals. Even in the early 20th century, zoologists had little information on the rorquals, the largest animals to have ever inhabited our planet. For technical reasons they had never been hunted until the present century.

It would be very risky to attempt to identify with certainty when whale hunting began. First, a definition of "whale hunting" is needed. If this includes the ability to retrieve and use parts of whales that have been accidentally stranded on the shore, then historical documents clearly show that it has been going on for many thousands of years. But if, as in the present study, whale hunting means a systematic attempt to attack and capture the bigger whales on the high seas, then it can only have been going on for a few centuries. It is difficult to be more accurate than this because the imprecise terminology makes it impossible to know which cetacean species were being hunted by the peoples of antiquity and by the Norsemen and the Normans before 1000 A.D. Perhaps comparative linguistics will one day provide some answers.

Whale hunting in the strict sense definitely existed in the Middle Ages. It continued in its traditional form until the mid-19th century, which marks the beginning of the modern history of whaling. During this time the whale has been hunted by many: the Eskimos, the Amerindians, the Scots, the Germans, the Norwegians, the Japanese and the French of the northern coasts of France. However, four peoples have been far more active than any others: the Basques, both French and Spanish; the English; the Dutch and the Americans. This study considers what led these people to hunt whales, and when and where they did so. In each chapter a few paragraphs describe whaling technology, with the exception of the chapter on the Basques, whose technology will be analysed in detail in a later study.

PRECURSORS OF THE WHALE HUNTERS

Whale hunting did not appear spontaneously among the Basques, the English, the Dutch and the Americans. The methods these nations employed were the product of empirical knowledge acquired over thousands of years, and therefore a brief glance at the earlier periods is useful.

Whales have been hunted by a great variety of peoples since earliest times. Whale hunting is mentioned in the Bible, in ancient writings, and even in mythology. Well-known writers like Aristotle and Pliny mentioned it long before it became a well-organized industry.

Prehistoric Times

It would appear that humans first learned about whales when they cut up beached specimens. A beached whale has always been regarded by coastal peoples as a magnificent gift from nature. In *Aventures d'un voyageur en Australie* Perron d'Arc describes how Australian tribes celebrated such an event,[1] which provided not only food, but also oil, clothing, tools, construction materials and even weapons, such as the knives and small harpoons found in Jutland and at Skara Brae in the Orkneys. Archaeologists have even discovered adzes in the Orkneys, which is surprising, to say the least, in a region where there are no trees. According to Childe, these adzes were used to cut up whales. The number of bones present is not great enough, however, to allow us to suggest an organized whale-hunting industry.[2]

The benefits they derived from beached whales quickly led hunters not to wait for chance finds but to provoke them, by attacking whales out in the water or forcing them onto shore. This was quite daring, considering the equipment available in the Neolithic period 8000 years ago, although it is not altogether surprising since hunters are known to have attacked mammoths with flint tools and spears as early as the Palaeolithic period. Surprisingly realistic cave paintings at Roddoy in Norway show Neolithic whaling methods.[3] The hunters went out in long, very light, short-oared kayaks consisting of a wooden framework covered from end to end with sewn hides. In preparation for the attack, the boats were arranged in a semi-circle about the quarry. Then came the attack, each hunter planting a harpoon in the animal's body. When it was dead, barbed harpoons were sunk into its flesh in order to tow the catch ashore. Further evidence of whale hunting at this time comes from kitchen-middens containing the bones of porpoises, killer whales and pilot whales, and from the marks left by weapons or tools on the skeletons. The flesh was consumed either fresh or dried, and it is still used in this way as animal fodder in the Faeroe Islands. The oil provided light and warmth; the membrane surrounding the liver was made into a drumhead; the intestines were used for sewing skins; the baleen plates could be moulded into any shape once heated; the sinews were used to bind tools or weapons to shafts; the bones became boat timbers, tool handles, saddle frames, basins, dye pots, combs and even rafters for dwellings; finally, the skin was used to make leather clothes and rope.

Whale hunting in Norway in prehistoric times was practised mainly because climatic conditions precluded agriculture and forced the people to take their food from the sea. Such conditions also existed in Greenland, where researchers have recently found remains of old Eskimo villages containing structures made out of the bones of whales.[4] The Mongol tribes of Sakhalin Island off the shores of Japan hunted whales in kayaks. The inhabitants of the Aleutian Islands and Spitzbergen dipped their harpoons in a poison (probably a derivative of aconite) that made any wound fatal. Even today in some of the fjords of Norway, blood poisoning is induced by shooting rusted arrows that have been dipped in the blood of whales killed previously.

Amongst all these peoples, whale hunting involved rituals and beliefs that were sometimes quite complex. Every catch meant a great feast, and everywhere the products of the hunt acquired great value, for example whales' teeth in the Fiji Islands of the South Pacific, some of which were given to Queen Elizabeth II during her 1953 visit.

Antiquity

The people of ancient civilizations engaged in whale hunting, but it is not yet possible to determine whether they hunted the larger whales on the high sea, despite statements to this effect by some writers and despite the detailed descriptions we have of the animals.[5] Two sources appear to contradict each other, or at any rate are hard to reconcile. On the one hand, the best-informed writers, like Aristotle and Pliny, display their ignorance on the subject of whales by stating that whales are 200 metres long by 100 metres across, and that they swam upriver in Arcadia. Pliny's story of the capture of a large beached whale by the Emperor Claudius clearly shows that such catches were rare,[6] and Pliny's list of 42 types of oil does not include whale oil. On the other hand, certain cuneiform texts suggest that the Phoenicians may have hunted whales (including sperm whales) several centuries before Pliny's time. In 1100 B.C., according to one text, the Assyrian king Tiglath-pileser sailed on a Phoenician whale-hunting ship. The author of the document speaks of an animal named the *nakhiru,* meaning "blower." The story of the expedition is engraved on an obelisk in the British Museum. It reads: "in ships of Arvad [the king] rode; a blower in the great sea [the Mediterranean] he slew. Wild bull destructive and fine."[7] A bas-relief that the Assyrian king Ashurnasirpal (884-860 B.C.) had sculpted on the gates of Ashur shows two sperm whales. Although these sources say nothing about the Phoenicians' whaling methods, ships or oil-extraction procedures, they do indicate the uses made of the catch: artists made objects of ivory, which they also called "bone of whale," and these objects were exported, along with the oil, to various foreign lands, especially Egypt. Phoenician whale hunting is also attested to by a tribute they had to pay to their conquerors, the Assyrians; part of the tribute consisted of whale teeth, which would appear to show that whale hunting was a common activity of the Phoenicians: "Teeth of blowers, the produce of the sea, their tribute I received."[8]

How do what appear to be Phoenician whale hunting and trade in whale products square with the almost total silence of Aristotle and Pliny several centuries later? The most plausible answer would be that, for reasons that remain unclear, the technique of whale hunting was lost. It is possible that the Phoenicians' successors did not possess the technical and navigating knowledge required, or that some religious practice led to the decline: the fresco of Queen Maragon at Knossos in Crete, as well as numerous examples of Minoan and Mycenean pottery, attest to the fact that the Greeks had deep respect for dolphins in particular, and even venerated them.

The practice of hunting the bigger whales, whether or not it existed at the time of the Phoenicians, had disappeared by the time of the Greeks and Romans. Only a few isolated groups still caught the smallest species: for example, the inhabitants of the island of Cythera used sinews of whales, but not dolphins, in making musical instruments and machines of war.[9] Around the same time, the Ichthyophagi and the Shihuh of Cape Musandam, on the south shore of the Strait of Hormuz at the entrance to the Persian Gulf, used whale jaws as door frames and the ribs as rafters for their homes.[10] However, there is no proof that they hunted the big whales; probably they used the skeletons of accidentally beached animals.

The first centuries of the Christian era are marked by almost total silence on the subject of whale hunting. Only Oppian mentions that whales were hunted in the second century, with a chain and a hook baited with a cow's shoulder.[11]

The Normans

Documentary evidence of whale hunting does not really begin until the end of the first millenium, with the invasion of northern France by the Normans. The Normans were a Norse people who appear to have brought the practice of whale hunting with them from Scandinavia, or at any rate to have revived the practice in Normandy. The terms of endowment specifying the income of the Abbot of Saint-Denis mention the *crassus piscis*, a term normally used to designate whales capable of providing blubber.[12] The documents also speak of *valseta*, apparently from the Scandinavian *hval-setr*, an expression applied to the fishing ground or shore establishment. Does this mean that whale hunting was practised on the coasts of Normandy in Carolingian times? If so, it may go back to the 7th century, when Saint Philibert selected Jumièges as the site for his monastery because oil for lamps and food for the monks could be obtained from the marine animals there.[13] Around 875 a text entitled *Miracula Sancti Vedasti* describes whale hunting by mariners belonging to the fleets of various monasteries in the Pas-de-Calais area. The story shows that the hunt was communally organized; participants paid a fee into a "contubernium" (a sort of co-operative society) and agreed to share the catch.[14] It seems clear from the description that the hunt was an organized activity intended to catch the largest possible number of whales. This is also clearly indicated in three texts from the period of ducal supremacy. A charter from the priory of Héauville on Cape La Hague describes the restrictions on whaling at that port. Another charter, from the capitulary of Saint-Etienne de Caen, describes the operations of a whalers' society at Dives-sur-Mer. Finally, there is a narrative by Raoul Tortaire of a whaling expedition in which he took part on the Bessin coast between the Orne River and Port-en-Bessin around the year 1115. The hunt took place in the shallow waters in wintertime. The hunters used nets and whaling boats (called by the Scandinavian name *walmanni*) to surround the whales. They pursued them, making a lot of noise — whence the French expression *pêcher à cri et à hue*, "to fish while raising a great hue and cry" — and struck them with three-pronged spears. Once wounded, the animals were hauled onto the beach and cut up.[15] Norman law distinguished whales captured in the course of a hunt *à cri et à hue* from those that were beached *à verec*, that is, accidentally. In the latter case the entire catch belonged to the duke, whereas in the former case only a symbolic portion was given to him. This Scandinavian-inspired law is also to be found in a Danish text from Jutland, which granted to the king all the fish a man could not carry.[16]

Whale hunting was practised only in places with large beaches, like the estuaries of the Saire, the Dives, the Seine and the Bresle, where the prey could be forced ashore. Catches must have been fairly large since whalemeat was already being exported from Rouen to London in 979.[17] A law of Ethelred II sets the taxes on such imports of *crapois* (probably porpoise).[18] The king of England appears even to have abolished the tax on transported goods in order to encourage the trade in whalemeat — further evidence that there must have been regular, organized hunts, since the trade would not be based only on accidental beachings.

The Icelanders and Norwegians

During this same period, but further to the north, the Icelanders and the ancestors of the Norwegians also hunted for whales. The Norwegians used squat, clinker-built ships of oak on a frame of curved timbers that been deliberately grown that way. The planking was bolted and riveted together from the inside, and then lashed to the frames with withes made from roots. The caulking was made of cow hair. The ships had no keel or rudder post; they were steered by a large outside oar. They had sails, but only fore and aft oars, for use in entering ports. They displaced 50 tons and carried up to 15 tons of cargo. There was a forecastle to shelter the sleeping mariners, and a small poop deck connected to it by a covered passage along either side of the keel. The crew consisted of 50 to 60 men and women. The ships were called *knorr* or *kaup-skip*, meaning "trading ship."[19]

The method used for hunting was to make a great deal of noise in order to drive the whales into one of the many fjords along the Norwegian coast. The entrance to the fjord was then blocked with large-mesh nets. The purpose of this was not to keep the whales in but to frighten them and thus force them up onto the land at the head of the fjord. According to one writer, the Norwegians killed the whales with a large ballista, or sort of giant crossbow, which shot an extremely heavy harpoon that bore a metal tip mounted on a wooden shaft eight centimetres in diameter, and was connected to a powerful winch.[20] It does seem improbable that such equipment was actually used: it is hard to imagine the hunters repeatedly launching harpoons at a whale, an ineffective and exhausting operation because of the inaccuracy, slowness and weight of such a huge machine. It would be more logical to assume that the whales were killed with arrows soaked in the dried blood of previous catches, in the manner of the prehistoric hunters. Over the course of a few days the resulting contamination would make the whales very sick, and they could then easily be killed and hauled onto shore, this probably being the purpose of the winch.[21]

The Flemish

The best-known whaling expedition during this period was probably that of Othere on behalf of England in 890. According to the authenticated story of his voyage, as reported to King Alfred, the Flemish explorer sailed along the Norwegian coast "so far north as commonly the whale-hunters used to travel." He was searching for "horse-whales, which had bones of very great value for their teeth.... These whales are much less than other whales being only 5 ells long." He added that the best whales were to be found in his own country, "of which some were 48, some 50 ells long," and he claimed that, with five companions, he killed 60 of these large whales in only two days.[22]

Many historians have been confused by this text, and there is still no general agreement on how to interpret it. Clearly, six people did not kill 60 big whales in two days. Even with the most modern equipment, such a feat would be impossible. The problem lies either in the interpretation given to the word "ell" or in the figure "60." The ell has not been precisely defined. According to Charles Scammon, it was 90 centimetres, except to the Flemish, for whom it was 67.5 centimetres.[23] If this latter equivalence is applied to the Othere story, then the "horse-whales" are probably walruses about 3.3 metres long (normal for this species). But the large whales mentioned in the story would be 34 metres long — the length of a large blue whale! This cannot possibly be right. The great rorquals could not have been hunted before the late 19th century because they swim so fast, they are extraordinarily strong, and they do not float once dead. Schreiner suggests that in fact the ell was 30 centimetres.[24] The largest whales mentioned in the story would then be 15 metres long – more or less the length of a Greenland or Biscayne whale. The whales described by Othere cannot have been Greenland whales since these are not found as far south as Flanders. Also, according to the Norwegian *Kongespeiler* of 1250, sailors at this time were afraid of the *slettibaka*, which is apparently the old name for the Greenland whale.[25] This leaves the Biscayne whale, but then there is the problem that, using Schreiner's figure, the walruses would be only 1.5 metres long, well below average. The only thing that is clear in Othere's story is that in the 9th century the Flemish were hunting whales that were nine to ten times bigger than Norwegian "horse-whales."

If they were indeed Biscayne whales, it is not possible that 60 were caught in two days. According to William Scoresby, the famous English whaler and scientist, the number 60 is an error of interpretation or transcription. After examining the original text, he concluded that the number should be read as 6.[26] He says that linguists substituted *syxtig* (60) for *syxta* (6). With 9th-century techniques it would have been quite possible to catch six Biscayne whales in two days. The general conclusion to be drawn from Othere's story, then, is that the Flemish were indeed hunting the bigger whales in the 9th century.

Returning to the Norwegians, according to the saga of Olaf Tryggveson, they hunted the whale (which they regarded as a fish) more for its meat than for its oil.[27] Specifically, this was true of the colonists who were with Eric the Red in Greenland. They also valued the ivory from the teeth, as well as the bladder and intestines that when inflated, served as floats. Walrus and narwhal were kept for trading purposes because of the great value attached to them in Europe. According to some legends, it was while pursuing whales that the Vikings reached the shores of America around the year 1000.[28]

The Germans

According to Albertus Magnus in *De animalibus*, whales were harpooned from three-man boats. In the belief that the animals were sensitive to "music," the boats assembled in one place and the hunters played on kettledrums and other instruments. When the whales "lent an ear," harpoons attached to long ropes were thrown, and then the hunters moved away as fast as they could. The animals dived, but because they were wounded they soon showed signs of exhaustion. The hunters then formed a circle around them, and finished them off with pikes.[29]

Before 1000 A.D., the Norse peoples were practising whale hunting in the North Atlantic. Some of them hunted only the smaller species, while others went after the bigger ones. They used the various parts of the whale for a wide variety of purposes; in no case do they appear to have hunted whales for any reason other than survival or domestic consumption. Whale hunting among most of these peoples reached its peak between the 10th and 12th centuries. Then the Basques — a people few in numbers who also hunted whale along the shores of the Bay of Biscay — for the first time made whaling an international industry. The real story of whale hunting in the North Atlantic begins with this hardy, inventive, sea-going race. The nations who hunted whales after the time of the Basques would be indebted to them.

THE BASQUES

The Basques in the Bay of Biscay

Because the history of Basque whale hunting has yet to be written,[1] we do not know when the practice began. Researchers have found harpoons in the Basque region dating from the Palaeolithic but these do not exceed 30 centimetres in length.[2] In historic times the Basques were sending oil to light the monastery at Jumièges in 670,[3] but there is no proof that what they were sending was whale oil.

The first known documents providing evidence of whale hunting date from the 11th and 12th centuries. In 1059 a fee in the form of a portion of the animal had to be paid on whales caught in the mouth of the Adour River in France.[4] In Spain, fishing was an appurtenance of the Crown under section XI of "Las Partidas," though the king did grant fishing rights (keeping a portion of the profits for himself) so that people would settle in the coastal towns and thus provide better protection for the country. In 1150 King Sancho the Wise of Navarre granted the town of Saint Sebastian certain rights to store whalebone; the inhabitants then had to pay only two dineros.[5] Alphonse VIII of Castille and Ferdinand III would later extend this right to the towns of Fontarabie in 1203, Motrico and Guetaria in 1204 and Zaraux in 1237.[6] Finally, on 6 September 1199, King John of England granted Vital de Bielle, the governor of Bayonne, and his heirs the authority to take 50 Angevin pounds annually from the product of the sale of the first two whales caught by the hunters at Biarritz.[7]

Even the oldest of these documents shows that the Basques had already been hunting the bigger whales for many years. Did they learn to do it from the Normans, who had brought the skill with them from Scandinavia and invaded Gascony in the 11th century, or did they begin doing it by themselves? Although they may indeed have learned from foreigners, it would be an exaggeration to say that they copied Scandinavian methods. The deep fjords where the Norwegians forced the whales ashore did not exist in the Basque country, and so the hunters had to learn to catch the animals out at sea. This required such great changes that it is justifiable to speak of a native Basque technique. According to one view, this was developed in the 9th century in the course of chasing off whales that regularly destroyed fishing nets. Finding that the whale was a timid and inoffensive creature, the Basques took the risk of hunting it with harpoons, and in this way they discovered its immense value.[8] The new source of income was especially welcome since the land in the Basque country, especially the Labourd region, was sterile, and only fishing could bring in any profit.

Within the space of a century, the Basques mastered the art of whale hunting, moving ahead of all their North European competitors.

The decline of the whale hunt in Northern Europe coincided with the peak of Basque whaling activity in the 13th and 14th centuries. For several centuries, the whale catch was to provide significant revenues throughout the Basque country, from Saint-Jean-de-Luz in France to Cantabria in Spain. There is abundant evidence for this in archives in Biarritz and Lequeitio in particular. At the time many fruits and vegetables were still unknown, and fish was a nutritional staple. The year contained 166 days when meat-eating was prohibited by religious custom, thus reinforcing the importance of fish in the diet. Cod was, of course, popular, but whale, considered to be a fish, was also much in favour in those areas where it was hunted or to which it was transported. It was so highly valued that the Basques even established consulates in Holland, Denmark and England to encourage sales. The blubber was sold in Paris under the name *craspois* or *lard de carême* (lenten fat). Prior to the later period between the 12th to 14th centuries, when the Basques would outfit their ships for lengthy expeditions, all parts of the whale were used. The flesh was food for the poor and for ships' crews;[9] the oil was used for lighting and as a lubricant, in the preparation of soap, wool, leather and paint; the whalebone went into making clothes, decorations, such as the plumes of knights' helmets, women's hats, corset stays, snuffboxes, chair springs, hairbrush bristles, and skirt hoops; the vertebrae, ribs and jaws became seats, fence pickets, beams, and votive offerings placed at either side of church doors, and they were even used in masonry still visible in many medieval buildings in Bayeux;[10] the excrement was used to tint fabrics red,[11] and in northern Spain the blubber was used as a condiment — whence the name "whale-fat-soup eaters," applied to the inhabitants of Tolosa. All of these whale products were sold in France, Spain, Flanders and England. In *La vie privée des Français*, d'Aussy cites a 13th-century manuscript according to which whale tongue was sold in markets at Bayonne, Ciboure and Biarritz.[12] Tongue was a delicacy reserved for the clergy and the monarch; in 1565 two quintals of whale tongue were presented to Charles IX and Catherine de Médicis.

In the 13th and 14th centuries so many whales were being taken that the church and the royal authorities saw in the whale hunt a means of increasing their revenues. Up until the mid-12th century, under the provisions of a clause in the Judgments of Oléron, the Basques had been exempted from payment of duties; whatever they paid to their lords was a gift. The clause was revoked by Henry II, king of England (1154-1189) and duke of Guyenne. The Basque archives contain dozens of examples of taxes and fees on the whale trade beginning at this time. In Biarritz a regulation of 1268 set the duties that mariners had to pay the seneschal for each whale they caught;[13] in Guetaria it was the custom that the first whale caught each season be presented to the king, who usually returned half of it;[14] and in 1270, during the period of English domination, the future King Edward I confirmed the right of the inhabitants of Anglet and Biarritz to hunt whale in return for a payment that went toward the fortifications of Bayonne.[15] In 1338, during the reign of Edward III, this payment was set at six pounds per whale.[16] The proceeds must have been considerable since the king bequeathed the right to collect the money to Pierre de Puyanne as compensation for funds advanced to outfit a fleet.[17] According to the rent collector of Bayonne cathedral, on 20 February 1261 the town's governor, Vital de Bielle, awarded the tithe on all the whales from the port of Biarritz to the parish of Sainte-Marie and to the chapter of the cathedral.[18] Similar tithes existed in most of the Spanish Basque whaling towns.

There is further evidence of the importance of whale hunting in the Basque country during this period. The towns of Fontarabie, Guetaria, Motrico, Lequeitio, Bermeo and Castro Urdiales all have whales on their coats of arms, which suggests that they were known for whaling. Many houses had a room on the ground floor set aside for melting blubber. As late as the early 20th century the remains still existed of towers and lookouts from which the Basques would scan the sea for whales.

In the 13th and 14th centuries whales were hunted on the open sea in the Bay of Biscay.[19] The methods that were practised until the mid-19th century date from this period. One of the great advantages the Basques had was to be able to watch hundreds of whales moving southward down the coast every year, beginning at the autumnal equinox and continuing throughout the winter. The species in question was *Eubalaena glacialis*, now among the rarest in the world, and better known as the black right whale or Biscayne whale. At the time the Basques were hunting them, the French called this species *baleine des Sardes*, the Norwegians *nord-kaper*, the Icelanders *sléttbakùr* and the Basques *sardako*, meaning "whale living in a group." They were slow and inoffensive, and under 20 metres in length. They were ideal quarry for the hunters, as compared to the species that were too fast for their boats, or too strong to be caught with the equipment available at the time. Most important, they would float after death, unlike the rorquals, so the hunters could tow them to shore or to the boat for cutting up.

This type of whale hunting disappeared from the Bay of Biscay beginning in the 15th century. For some reason not yet understood, the Basque hunters moved out into the Atlantic at that time. The most generally accepted theory is that intensive hunting between the 12th and 15th centuries had made whales scarce in the waters off the Basque country. There is as yet no satisfactory proof of this view, and in fact it would appear unlikely that the whales had become scarce, given the technical means then in use. Even had the catch along the Basque coast decreased in the 15th century, this could not possibly be because of over-hunting. In comparison to the modern-day hunt, Basque catches were insignificant. Archival research has shown that none of the communities actively enagaged in the hunt ever killed more than six whales in a season; even in the best years all of the Basques together would never have caught more than 100 whales. According to the archives at Lequeitio, only 48 whales were taken between 1517 and 1661.[20] It is true that the whale is supposed to have abandoned the coasts of Spain by this time, but even assuming that during the height of the whaling era in the Bay of Biscay catches were higher than those mentioned above, it is unlikely the hunt would have affected the size of whale stocks. The English, Dutch and American whalers who took over the whaling scene in the 17th century caught hundreds of times more whales than the Basques took between the 12th and 15th centuries, and yet it took them over a century to reduce stocks of sperm whales and Greenland whales to the point where expeditions became unproductive and the species' survival was threatened. In favour of the theory of a decline in stocks, there is a document written in 1710 by traders in the Labourd area. According to it, the Basques had been hunting whales off their shores since time immemorial, but because the animals had become scarce, they stopped "until the use of the compass and the jacob staff had become known."[21] Of course, this document was written three centuries after the Basques supposedly stopped coastal whaling. It is possible that the number of Biscayne whales was less than that of other species since it was slow and inoffensive and therefore more vulnerable, but no statistics are available to back this up.

There are more plausible explanations for the Basques abandoning coastal whaling after the mid-15th century. A change in the currents, or some other factor, may have led to climatic changes in the bay, forcing the whales to seek a more suitable habitat. There are examples in the case of other European marine species at this same time. Cod, which had been abundant along the coasts of Spain, moved westward toward the end of the Middle Ages,[22] and according to the chronicles, herring deserted the Baltic in 1473.[23] The same could have happened to the Biscayne whale, forcing the hunters to follow it.

It is also possible that after being hunted for three centuries along the shores of the bay, the whales instinctively moved away from the dangerous area. They may have continued to live in the bay over the winter, but most of them may have stayed away from the shore, obliging the hunters to follow them out onto the high seas. The hunters who did not possess the technical and financial means to do so were satisfied to just go after the rare specimens that ventured near shore. Such a state of affairs would not be unique in the history of whaling; it was to occur in Spitsbergen in the 17th century.

A further possibility is that, encouraged by their success during the winter along the coasts of France and Spain, the Basques set off to find out where the whales congregated so that they could hunt them all year round. This was the view expressed by Cleirac in *Us et coutumes de la mer*:

> The great profits, and the facility with which the inhabitants of Capbreton near Bayonne and the Basques of Guyenne were able to catch the whales, were lures that made them bold enough to pursue their quest out onto the Ocean, to every latitude and longitude. And to this end they outfitted their ships, to search for the customary abode of these colossal creatures.[24]

The emerging mercantile capitalism created favourable conditions for naval construction, which requires great investments of funds, while the taking of Constantinople from the Turks in 1453 opened up new trade routes. The Basques — already good navigators, to judge by the fact that Edward II entrusted them to bring Isabel of France to England — must certainly have taken advantage of these economic developments.[25]

The Basques in North America

Whether because of a shortage of whales causing by excess hunting, or because they wanted to increase their revenues, in the 15th century, and perhaps earlier, the Basques began to move up the Atlantic coast of Europe in search of whales. The move northward is additional evidence in favour of the view that they left the Bay of Biscay because they wanted to hunt whale all year long. The whales frequented the more northern waters before moving down to the Bay of Biscay in the autumn. The Basques apparently decided to extend the hunting season but still stay near their markets in northern Europe.

The dates and destinations of their expeditions are not known with certainty. Some writers claim that the Basques reached Scotland in the 14th century[26] and Iceland in the year 1412.[27] The latter claim is based on a document that announces the arrival in Groenfjord, in the Gulf of Grunder, of 20 Basque ships equipped for whale hunting. This is quite plausible, since Iceland has ancient customs of Basque origin, such as the making of a barley-and-water drink called *cilia*.[28] Once in Iceland, it was only a step to America for these excellent navigators.

There can be no doubt that the Basques did indeed come to North America. The tombstones at Placentia in Newfoundland and the ovens on Ile aux Basques and Ile du Havre Mingan in the St. Lawrence are only a few among numerous pieces of evidence that the Basques were here at a certain point in our history. What is not so certain, and much debated, is when they came.

The earliest date given for the Basques' arrival in North America is 1372 — a century before Christopher Columbus's discovery of the new continent.[29] In Branco's atlas of 1436 there is a land in the far western Atlantic bearing the name "Scorafixa" or "Stocafixa." Several other mid-15th-century maps also show islands in the western Atlantic that could be Newfoundland. They bear the name "Stockfish" or "Bacalao"; the latter, which means "cod" in Spanish, would later be applied exclusively to Newfoundland.[30] Finally, the previously noted document of 1710 states that at the time when "the use of the compass and the jacob staff became known" (i.e., the 15th century), the Basques set out on the western route in search of whales and arrived in Newfoundland, where they found tremendous quantities of whale and cod.[31] A few other documents also exist that suggest that America was discovered by the Basques at least a century before Columbus came in 1492.

Several writers of the 16th and 17th centuries concluded from these sources that the Basques had indeed discovered America before Columbus. Among them are Guillaume Postel (*Merveilles des Indes et du Nouveau Monde*, which appeared in 1553), followed by Rondelet, Pierre de l'Ancre, Corneille Wysfler, Anthoine Magin, Father Fournier and Étienne Cleirac (*Us et coutumes de la mer*, first published in 1647). Fournier the elder even claims that Alphonse Sanchez de Huelva was brought to Madeira by a storm on his return from Newfoundland, and that he died in 1492 after revealing his secret to Columbus, who promptly departed with a crew of Basque sailors including the famous

Jean de Biscaye.[32] If this is true, it is certainly odd that Columbus arrived in the West Indies rather than in Newfoundland.

Other writers believe that such claims are without foundation and that the Basque voyages took place after Columbus. This is the view of René Bélanger, who has made a study of the evidence for a Basque presence in the St. Lawrence Estuary.[33] One thing that is certain is that before 1493 no map or document or story mentions America in any definite way. Because 15th-century cartographic and toponymic practices were imprecise, it is not certain that the lands mentioned in the western Atlantic really were America. Yet common sense requires that the experts explain what else they might be. Unlike other peoples, the Basques do seem not to have engaged in the practice of officially claiming possession of lands they visited in the course of their expeditions. They were neither explorers nor colonizers. They were hunters who wanted to keep their routes secret and were thus very reticent about writing down anything that might make it easier for their competitors.[34]

Nevertheless, the Basques were certainly frequenting what are now Canadian waters by the first half of the 16th century and were finding large numbers of whales.[35] Documents from the 1550s show unequivocally that in the ports of Biarritz, Capbreton, Pasajes, Renteria, Saint-Jean-de-Luz, Saint Sebastian and Ciboure many ships were being outfitted every year to go after whale and cod in the new lands. The first definite reference to the existence of this activity in Labrador dates from 1554, though the *Grand Insulaire et pilotage*, written around 1550 by the cosmographer André Thévet, says that there is an island near Tadoussac (Thadoyzeau) where Spaniards and men from Bayonne come every year to hunt for whale.[36]

There is definite evidence of a Basque influence on the Amerindian peoples. A French Basque document in the city archives of Saint-Jean-de-Luz says that the Basques established trade relations with the indigenous peoples right from the start, and specifically with the Eskimos. Since the languages of these two people were, of course, different, they established a sort of lingua franca composed of Basque and two Amerindian languages. "The persons who established settlements in the French colonies in Canada and in the northern part of Acadia found this language long-established when they first arrived...."[37] This is confirmed by Marc Lescarbot in his *Histoire de la Nouvelle-France*, and by Father Charles Lalemant who writes, in his relation of 1626, that the Indians called the sun *Jesus*, a name he says they had gotten from the Basques.[38] There is no reason, however, to think that the Basques and the Amerindians spoke a common language. The resemblance between Basque and Algonquin in particular has led some who lack an actual knowledge of these languages to believe that they are one and the same. In fact, the Basques and Algonquins may have communicated with a few frequently used words learned by both sides; the Basques left one of their own behind with the Indians in 1636, presumably to learn the language.

Place-names provide further evidence of the Basque presence. Newfoundland in particular has a large number of place-names of Basque origin.

The peace treaty between France and Spain, signed at Cateau-Cambrésis in 1559 and sealed by the marriage of Philip II and Elizabeth of Valois, was a factor in the growing number of ships that went whaling in the 1560s. Around 1570 the Basques sent out 50 whaling ships to the new lands.[39] In a letter to Hakluyt dated 13 November 1578, Anthony Parkhurst states that he had made four voyages to Newfoundland and that on each occasion he met a hundred or so Spanish ships fishing for cod, and 30 or 40 others hunting for whale.[40] To this number must be added those operating in the St. Lawrence and in Labrador. Labrador was now humming with activity from June till autumn. In 1705 Augustin Le Gardeur de Tilly, sieur de Courtemanche, described the port in Red Bay:

> It was also in this harbour that the whales were once hunted. According to the Savages, the Eskimos made the Europeans leave. One can still see the furnaces where the oil was made, and the bones of the whales which lie on the shore like overturned tree trunks one atop the other. They must have killed more than two or three thousand, to judge from the quantity of bones which we counted: 90 heads in just one place, of enormous size.[41]

In 1579 Captain Martin de Hoyarsabal of Ciboure named this bay Boytus.[42] A few years earlier the name "las partes de Terra nueva" had been replaced by "la Provincia de Terranova," which suggests that the Spanish Basques were already dominant in Labrador. Since the voyage of Joro Fernandes in 1500, Labrador had been distinguished from the island of Newfoundland, a fact confirmed by a memoir of Bernardino de Mendoza who was asked by the Spanish king in 1578 to inquire into a voyage the English had made "to the country called Labrador, which joins Newfoundland where the Biscay men go in search of whale."[43]

In the late 16th century the golden age of whale hunting in Labrador suddenly came to an end.[44] The centre of activity moved west to the St. Lawrence, extending upstream of Tadoussac, and the hunt was now dominated by the French Basques. In June 1626 Champlain says that he met Basques who had been hunting whale at Sept-Iles.[45] Such activity continued, albeit on a limited basis, until the 18th century. In the 1730s the Detcheverrys and Simon Darragory of Saint-Jean-de-Luz established a whaling station at Bon Désir near Tadoussac. In their report of 1735 to the minister, they say that they had captured nine humpback whales, one sperm whale and one of the smaller whales. Their efforts had yielded 145 quintals of oil. In 1736 the king granted them exclusive whaling rights for four years. This put them in conflict with the Fermiers du Domaine d'Occident company, and in 1738 they established themselves at Sept-Iles. Six years later they abandoned the hunt.[46] Some Canadians attempted to take up where they had left off, but were unsuccessful.

The reason for the gradual decline of Basque whaling activity along the coasts of North America is unclear. It began in the late 16th century for the Spanish Basques and in the early 17th for the French Basques. The main cause was the discovery in the early 17th century of new hunting grounds in Spitsbergen, but there are various opinions about why the Basques preferred Spitsbergen over their older whaling grounds in Canada.

21

In the second half of the 16th century and throughout the 17th century the Basques were often victims of wars between the great European powers. After the defeat of the Armada, Spain could no longer guarantee protection to its fishermen and whalers, and many ships were captured by enemy privateers and by pirates. Fees and high taxes, embargos, requisitioning of boats and crews, and the salt monopoly under Philip III and Philip IV led many whalers to join the boats going to Newfoundland from Saint-Jean-de-Luz. The French Basques fared no better. Between 1598 and 1627 they came into conflict with the companies that held the trade monopoly along the St. Lawrence River and Gulf. Numerous recorded confrontations show that from the early 17th century on the Basques no longer enjoyed complete freedom of action in the area. Perhaps they therefore decided that it was not worthwhile venturing so far from their own land.

The cod fishery may have been another reason for the decline of Basque whaling in North America. Once the Newfoundland cod banks were discovered, many fishermen chose to restrict their activities to cod fishing. A notable example was the Basques of Placentia. Cod-fishing was in many ways more profitable: it produced oil like the whale, but in addition, flesh that could be transported to Europe — a very important factor in an era when huge quantities of fish were consumed.

Bacqueville de La Potherie, Charlevoix and other writers have claimed that the Basques abandoned the whale hunt for the more lucrative and less dangerous fur trade.[47] The fact that the language of many Amerindian tribes has been influenced by Basque shows that there was contact. According to one account, around 1636 the Basques left a young boy with the Indians so that he would learn their language. Unfortunately, they ate him during the course of the winter.[48] Champlain mentions that in 1623 "a vessel of 50 or 60 tons had arrived in Tadoussac to hunt the whale ... and they had with them six to seven hundred écus worth of goods for trading."[49]

Another possible explanation is that the Basques, who mainly frequented the North Shore of the St. Lawrence, were chased away by the Eskimos, with whom they were not on very good terms. This, at any rate, was the view of several chroniclers of the early 17th century, including a Father Biard, who says that the conflict started when the Basques abducted the wife of an Eskimo chief "but they paid dearly for their dissoluteness, and not only them, but also the men of Saint Malo and many others have suffered because of them, and suffer greatly again every year."[50]

The departure of the Basques might also be explained in part by the available stocks of whales. It was not that they had become scarce in North America but rather that they were available in such great abundance in the bays of Spitsbergen where, according to Cleirac, "these colossal creatures swim and frolic in bands like carp in a fishpond."[51] Since they had never been hunted in this region, the whales were less fearful and thus easier to capture.

A final possible explanation is that the decline of Basque whaling in North America was simply a part of a general decline of fishing in the Basque country. This was quite certainly the case with the Spanish Basques, where signs of it began to appear after the death of Philip II in

1598. Not only was Spain no longer able to protect its fishermen, but also it was imposing heavier and heavier taxes on them. The role the Basques would play in Spitsbergen, and later in Davis Strait, suggests that their activities were already experiencing a slowdown when this new area opened in the early 17th century.

The Basques in Spitsbergen

The move from North America to Spitsbergen came too late to preserve what remained of the Basque whaling industry. In Spitsbergen (then called Greenland), the Basques came into conflict with the English and the Dutch, who at that time were just making their first appearance on the whaling scene. The competition — especially with the Dutch — was a factor in bringing Basque whaling to an end.

The whale hunt in Spitsbergen began in 1611, 15 years after the discovery of the island by the Dutchman Willem Barendszoo (better known as William Barents). In 1607 Henry Hudson had visited the island on behalf of the Muscovy Company and discovered large numbers of Greenland whales in the area. Three years later the company sent out its first ship — a 70-tonner under Captain Jonas Poole. The ship was not equipped for whaling because at that time the English, like the Dutch, were not yet taking an interest in the whale hunt. But it did not take long for the members of the Muscovy Company to grasp the potential. Being aware of their ignorance of whaling technique, they attempted to take advantage of the knowledge and experience of the Basques, who had been whaling for at least 500 years. Accordingly the company sent Nathaniel Wright to the Basque country to recruit hunters. His mission was to last 14 years.[52]

The first Muscovy Company expedition to Spitsbergen, in 1611, included six Basque hunters originally from Saint-Jean-de-Luz.[53] It was a failure. The following year the English tried again, using Basque harpooners, but this time they encountered Dutch and Basque expeditions headed respectively by Allen Sallowes and Nicholas Woodcocke, two former employees of the Muscovy Company.

In Spitsbergen the Basques were thus acting either on their own or as employees of the English or the Dutch. The English used Basques right from the start; Baffin called them "our whale strikers." In a letter of 1612, King James I of England asked the king of Spain for permission to hire Basques for English whaling expeditions.[54] The Dutch adopted a similar policy early. In 1613 the crews of two Dutch ships equipped for whaling included 12 Basques: three harpooners, three whaleboat captains, and the rest experts at flensing and boiling.[55] As a form of recompense and encouragement, the Dutch are even said to have erected statues to the best Basque harpooners and captains. A memoir written in 1710 on the discovery of Newfoundland states: "One still sees such statues in Amsterdam, with the figures clothed in old Basque dress."[56] Cleirac says that while the Basques were indeed better hunters than the Dutch, the Dutch were better navigators; the Basques, he says, were more interested in "emptying a bottle of brandy or smoking tobacco than in careful work with an astrolabe, triangle, quadrant and jacob staff."[57] The policy of hiring Basques had the twin effect of enabling the Dutch and English to learn whaling techniques and of depriving the Basque fleet of many of their best men.

Basques who went to Spitsbergen on their own rather than as employees of the Dutch or English found themselves caught in the struggle between the two powers for control of whaling in the area. In 1613 the Spanish Basques sent eight ships to the island.[58] In that same year James I of England issued a charter granting the Muscovy Company exclusive fishing rights in Spitsbergen. All other countries, as well as Englishmen who were not members of the company, thus lost access to the island. The company made only one exception — for a ship from Saint-Jean-de-Luz. In 1614 Holland countered by forming the Noodsche Company. The Muscovy Company was unable to compete with it and agreed in the end to share the island's coasts with Holland, Denmark, Hamburg, France and the Basques.

In the 1620s the Dutch became the leading whaling power in Spitsbergen, finally eliminating all competitors. Once they had learned whaling technique from the Basques, the Dutch drove them away, or at least this was what the *Compagnie française du Nord* claimed in a grievance to the high court in 1644:

> and when these Basques, as well as individual Frenchmen, claiming the same right there as other nations, tried to continue hunting and sending vessels, they were driven off, their ships were taken and they were imprisoned.[59]

Reacting to the Dutch attitude, the Basques pillaged whaling stations on the island of Jan Mayen in 1632.

From the 1630s on, the Basques had to hunt on the high seas since they now had no shore stations. Driven by necessity, they began to develop a new technique for transforming the blubber to oil. The method, developed by Martin Sopite, a Basque from Saint-Jean-de-Luz, made it possible to cut out and boil the blubber on board ship, thus making Basque whaling expeditions completely independent of land-based stations. This enabled them to exploit two new whaling areas as soon as they were excluded from Spitsbergen: one between Spitsbergen and present-day Greenland, and the other a place off Finland that they called Sarde. In the mid-17th century the towns of Saint-Jean-de-Luz, Bayonne and Ciboure were outfitting about 50 200- to 300-ton ships for whaling.[60]

Despite interdiction by the king in 1634, the Basques continued to work for the Dutch throughout the 17th century, as well as going out on their own expeditions. According to a publication of 1666, relations between Holland and Saint-Jean-de-Luz were still close during this period. The author says that in 1655 he had met men from Flanders in Saint-Jean-de-Luz who hired some 50 Basque whale hunters.[61]

Working for the Dutch, combined with strong Dutch competition, would soon lead to the decline of independent Basque activity.[62] In the early 18th century the ports of Saint-Jean-de-Luz, Ciboure and Bayonne outfitted only about 30 250-ton ships each.[63] The discovery of whales in Davis Strait around 1720 reinvigorated the industry, but only briefly. By the mid-18th century, irreversible decline had set in. A sign of this was what happened when a whale was stranded at Saint-Jean-de-Luz in 1764: the hunters went after it with implements that were rusty and in very poor condition. About 20 years later, whaling was only a memory among the French Basques. Thus ended at least seven centuries of continuous whaling activity.

Why, after such a glorious history, did Basque whaling come to a complete end in the late 18th century? The main reason is, of course, the appearance on the scene of the English and, in particular, the Dutch. Having learned to hunt whale from the Basques, the Dutch flooded Europe's markets, including the French market, with whale products. Their policy of selling at very low prices, often taking no profit, enabled them to capture Basque markets. Clearly, if Spain and France had done more to protect their whalers, the Basques would have been able to better withstand Dutch competition. Military protection at sea was already poor, and now the Basques got no protection or encouragement from their governments to deal with the onslaught of foreign products on the market. Quite the contrary: the Spanish and French governments made the situation worse by involving the whalers in prolonged wars, by levying high taxes, by embargoing boats, and by requisitioning boats and crews.

Another factor in the decline of Basque whaling was the sterility of the land in the Basque country. The Basques had to import most of the foodstuffs they put on their ships, and therefore the cost of outfitting a ship was greater. Because of Dutch competition they could not make up for this in the prices of whale products, and so their profit margins were small. Thus the hunters' income was reduced, and they emigrated, changed occupations, or went to work for the Dutch, who paid better. The scarcity of mariners to man the ships in turn reduced the size of ships and increased costs; it was more expensive to send out a small ship because the advantage of somewhat lower supply costs was lost through the greatly reduced catch.[64]

Further factors in the decline were disagreements among Basque shipowners concerning the hiring of crews, the French lag in naval construction, the administrative roadblocks set up by Spain, and the terrible state of the ports, which made ship movement perilous. The port of Bayonne, for instance, was continually being blocked by sandbanks that obstructed the entrance to the Adour River, obliging local shipowners to keep their ships at Pasajes over the winter. In the early 18th century the king effectively prohibited men from the province of Guipuzcoa from embarking on foreign ships. Each year French shipowners from Bayonne and Saint-Jean-de-Luz used to recruit about 200 oarsmen and harpooners from Guipuzcoa. The recruiting process followed an annual ritual: to do the most harm possible to the French whaling effort, the king of Spain would wait until the last minute before granting permission for the Spanish Basques to hire themselves out to the French owners, and the result was generally a poor catch. When the ships returned, a number of letters of excuse and justification would be exchanged between the Bayonne chamber of commerce and the delegates of the Spanish court, who would then remind the court of the services rendered to the Spanish by the French whalers, and of the bonds of fraternity that linked Basques on either side of the Pyrenees. Finally the king would promise to let the harpooners go without hindrance the next year, while the French owners would deplore the lack of skilled whalers in France. But the following year the same scenario would be repeated.[65] This made life complicated for the French owners, who had the capital but not the skilled labour. In a letter of 31 December 1729 the magistrates of Saint-Jean-de-Luz declared that "we will apply ourselves ... to training harpooners here at home, so that in due course we will be able to protect ourselves from the whims of our neighbours."[66] But this decision came too late.

THE ENGLISH

According to some sources, the beginnings of the English whale hunt go back to at least the 9th century.[1] This is based on Othere's report to King Alfred of his journey along the Norwegian coastline in 890, which he made on behalf of England.[2] While the story has been authenticated, it does not prove that the English were engaged in whale hunting at that time. There is nothing to show that Othere's voyage was made for the purpose of whaling, or even taking stock of the potential for whaling. Rather it would seem that his whaling exploits were just chance occurrences.

Even if the English had been whaling before 1000 A.D., all activity had probably stopped by the 13th century, for the Normans were supplying England with marine mammals at that time. Whalemeat was almost exclusively reserved for the king's use; in 1243 Henry III ordered the sheriffs of London to provide him with 100 chunks of whalemeat for his table.[3] In the 14th century, under acts of parliament passed in 1315 and 1324, all beached whales were deemed to be wreckage belonging to the king. They were cut in pieces and brought in carts to the royal kitchens. Sometimes the pieces were roasted on a spit, but most often they were boiled and served with peas.

It is not until the 16th century that historical documents provide the first evidence of whaling expeditions organized by the English. In 1594, Bristol shipowners outfitted some ships for whaling off Cape Breton. The *Grace*, in particular, apparently enjoyed great success. According to the evidence, this 35-ton barque, outfitted by a group of 12 men, left Bristol on 4 April 1594. It went to the Gulf of St. Lawrence and the western coast of Newfoundland. In St. George's Bay the crew found two large Basque ships that had been wrecked three years earlier with cargos totalling 700-800 baleen plates. Such expeditions, however, were episodic, or if they were regular there are no records to this effect.

The English in Spitsbergen

It was the discovery of Spitsbergen that really gave impetus to the English whale hunt.[4] The island was discovered on 19 June 1596 by the Dutchman William Barents, who was looking for the northern route to the Indies. Just as Cabot had reported the large cod stocks off Newfoundland a century earlier, so Barents now reported the great number of whales around Spitsbergen. On 1 May 1607 Henry Hudson left Gravesend aboard the 80-ton *Hopewell*.[5] Like Barents, he visited Spitsbergen and observed the large stocks of whale. At the time, however, neither Barents nor Hudson saw the whales as animals for hunting, even though Hudson was making his voyage for the Muscovy Company, which in 1576 (under the name Fellowship of English Merchants for Discovery of New Trades) had acquired a whale-hunting monopoly. The company was initially incapable of exploiting the northern waters, even though Robert Hitchcock had in 1580 drawn attention to the potential, but inferior ships, incompetent management and poor organization led, unsurprisingly, to failure.[6]

In the early 17th century the Muscovy Company had difficulty in maintaining its trading activity in the White Sea because of Dutch opposition. Hudson's expedition of 1607, intended to correct the situation, was not entirely successful, but the voyage was beneficial in that Hudson reiterated Barents's findings concerning the whale stocks. Three years later, mindful perhaps of Hitchcock's recommendations, the company decided to invest in whale hunting.

The first English expedition to Spitsbergen was in 1611. The previous year Jonas Poole had made a journey on the 70-ton *Amitié* to investigate Bear Island for the company. Although the English were now beginning to become acquainted with the Arctic, whale hunting was still a mystery to them, as evidenced by Poole's attitude when he came upon several whales but did not try to capture them because "the Basques were then the only people who understood whaling."[7] Poole was content to retrieve the baleen plates that had washed up on the beach.

Poole returned to Spitsbergen on the 50-ton *Elizabeth*, accompanied by the 160-ton *Mary Margaret* captained by Thomas Edge. They left Blackwall on 20 April 1611, and this time the ships were equipped for whaling. Poole's commission was explicit: after explaining that the company had spent a great deal of money to equip the ships, the commission ordered him to go to Spitsbergen to capture "a whale, or two or three."[8] To be as certain as possible of success, Poole took the precaution of taking along six Basque whalers from Saint-Jean-de-Luz, who had probably been hired by Nathaniel Wright when he went to the Basque country on behalf of the company to recruit skilled workers.

It was during this English expedition of 1611 that a whale was killed in the Arctic for the first time. Altogether 13 Arctic mammals were taken, but the expedition was a failure because the two ships were destroyed by ice. The crews and a portion of the cargo were saved by a ship from Hull.

In 1612 the Muscovy Company outfitted two new ships: the 160-ton *Whale* commanded by John Russell, and the 180-ton *Seahorse* under Thomas Edge. Both crews included Basques, and they took 17 whales and several walruses. The result was 180 barrels of oil and a net profit of 90 per cent of the original investment.[9]

But already the English were no longer alone at Spitsbergen. The lure of profit had encouraged other nations to try their luck. In 1612 the first Dutch ship arrived, captained by Allen Sallowes, who had worked for the Muscovy Company for 20 years but had been forced to leave England because of debts. Then a Basque ship from Saint Sebastian came under Nicholas Woodcocke, also a former company employee, who would later spend time in the Tower of London for this action. Also in the waters off Spitsbergen in 1612 were two ships from London and one from Hull, but employees of the Muscovy Company drove off all competitors without any justification.

In 1613 the company managed to extract from King James a charter that guaranteed them exclusive whaling rights in Spitsbergen. That same year, the company sent seven ships to the island, where they encountered two Dutch ships, 13 French and Spanish ships, and four English ships that were not sailing for the company. These ships let it be clearly understood that they had no intention of abiding by the king's charter. The company ships captured and brought to London the two Dutch ships with their cargos and whaling equipment; Dutch losses came to 130,000 guilders.[10] Three Basque ships were the only ones to obtain permission to hunt in Bell Sound, but in exchange they had to give the company eight whales, first rendering the blubber of some of them into oil. This stipulation shows that the English did not yet understand how to obtain the oil; they were trying to avoid being too harsh with those who were showing them how.

In 1614, in reaction to the policy of the Muscovy Company, the Dutch formed their own Noordsche Company. The two companies fought fiercely for control of whaling in Spitsbergen. The English whaling effort was quite productive: in 1616 and 1617 the company sent 22 ships and four pinnaces that brought back 3100 tons of oil.[11] The Dutch, meanwhile, sent out three or four warships each year to accompany their whaling ships.

A fresh confrontation occurred in 1618. This time the Dutch were victorious and the Muscovy Company had to agree to a division of Spitsbergen. The English kept the best ports on the island — Clock Bay, Safe Harbour, English Bay and English Harbour. The Dutch stations were further north, at North Bay, South Bay, Holland Bay and Amsterdam Island. The other nations whaling in Spitsbergen divided up the rest of the coast: the Danes were between the English and the Dutch at Danish Bay; the Hamburg whalers were in western Spitsbergen at a place called Hamburg Bay; and the Basques were in the far northern part of the island at Biscay Hook.

At the time, Greenland whales were present in great quantities off Spitsbergen. Never having been subjected to intensive hunting, they frequented the coastline, where they arrived in early summer. Whole schools of them would enter bays in search of food and remain there for some time.

The whaling ships generally carried crews of 30 or 40, along with 800 to 1000 64-gallon casks called cardels.[12] The ships were 250- to 400-tonners between 33 and 36 metres long and 6.5 and 8.5 metres wide. Hakluyt gives a list of the equipment needed on a 200-tonner with a crew of 55 in the early 17th century[13] (see Appendix D). It cost about £1200 to outfit such a ship.[14]

When they arrived in Spitsbergen, the English would select a bay frequented by the whales, lower anchor and strip their ship. The shore station would include housing, a workshop for the cooper, and the ovens for boiling blubber. The whaleboats sat upside down on the beach waiting to go out. Their number depended on the ship's tonnage: there would be six on a 200-tonner and three on a 60-tonner. Each boat had a crew of six: one harpooner, four oarsmen and a coxswain.

Everything had to be ready when the first whales arrived. Permanent observation posts were erected on the highest promontories along the coast. As soon as a whale was sighted, the watchkeeper would pass the word along to the next post, or directly to the whalers if possible. The signal was a basket hoisted to the top of a pole. The whalers would then put their boats into the water and set out after the whale. The technique learned from the Basques was used: a harpoon connected to the boat by a rope. If the whale was captured, it would be towed to shore, and the blubber and baleens removed. The blubber would be rendered into oil in the ovens, and the oil poured into the casks, which would then be floated out to the ship and hoisted on board. In a good season ships would sometimes be assigned solely to the transport of oil and baleen plates from Spitsbergen to England. In the early 17th century 95 per cent of the oil was used to make high-quality soap, and the rest was used for lighting.[15] (See Appendix E.)

Division of the island with the Dutch, and the founding of Smeerenberg by the Dutch in 1619, contributed to the decline the English whaling effort in Spitsbergen. The cost of outfitting a ship was unchanged, but the massive imports of oil into England had led to a drop in prices, so that profits were reduced and shipowners were hesitant to invest any more money in whaling. Also, since the English market could not absorb any more than 2000 tons of oil a year, it was essential to develop new markets,[16] but England's political interests opposed this. England even concluded oil import agreements with the Dutch, the main competitors of the English whalers.

Despite the great advantage obtained by the Muscovy Company in the division of the island, another important factor in the decline of English whaling there was the company's internal management. One among many points mentioned by Henry Elking in his history of the whale hunt in Spitsbergen is interference by the ships' captains. It must be borne in mind that each ship was headed by two men: the captain, in charge of navigation, and the "specksioneer," in charge of the hunt once the ship arrived at its destination. Though the captain was not a whaler, he would often ruin the season by exceeding his commission and interfering with the hunt. The way ships' captains were paid was also a factor in the decline: they were given fixed wages rather than a percentage of the catch, and therefore some of them, having decided that whaling was too demanding and too dangerous, preferred to spend their time ashore hunting, especially since any profits from this were exclusively theirs. In the end, the enormous cost of outfitting the ships, together with poor oil quality and inadequate maintenance of the equipment, completely swallowed up the company's reserves.[17]

Thus the worst enemies of the English after the Dutch were the English themselves. Their whaling effort actually lasted only a few years. By 1625 they were no longer able to compete with the Dutch. There was a regular decline in the average number of ships they sent out.[18] Around 1630 they were producing no more than 1100 tons of oil, about 50 per cent of local demand.[19] To improve the situation, they tried copying the Dutch and established a permanent station on the island, manned by prisoners awaiting the death sentence, but once these wretches saw Spitsbergen, they decided that immediate execution would be preferable to spending the winter there.

In the late 1630s whales became scarcer, staying away from the coastal stations. This required significant changes in hunting technique. The ships would have to remain constantly at sea, and the blubber could no longer be rendered near the whaling ground — the ships had to bring it back to their home ports in the raw state. This posed two problems. First, the raw blubber occupied more space than the corresponding amount of oil, so that expeditions were not as pofitable,[20] and second, the oil obtained from blubber boiled several months after the animal's death was of lower quality, so that certain industries, like the soap industry, ceased using it.

The English whaling industry, already in trouble, could not adapt to the new situation. The Dutch left to hunt whales in the waters to the east of present-day Greenland, but the English continued to work the bays of Spitsbergen. The resulting level of productivity and profitability was now never high enough that one could really speak of an industry: in 1669 a single ship, probably from Hull, went whaling,[21] whereas the Dutch fitted out 300-400 ships that year.[22]

In 1693 a fresh attempt was made to revive the English whaling effort, but once again it failed. The Company of Merchants of London Trading to Greenland, with 42 stockholders, had raised £40,000 and obtained a number of rights from the government to protect themselves. They came up against the same problems as the Muscovy Company, and went bankrupt after only nine years. After this, England abandoned the whale hunt and bought products from the Dutch.

The English in Davis Strait

By the early 18th century the whale stocks off Spitsbergen were exhausted and the stocks off the east coast of what is now Greenland were getting dangerously low. In 1719, while searching for new stocks, the Dutch discovered that large numbers frequented the Davis Strait. Within a few years over 350 ships were going there annually to hunt.[23] As was the case off eastern Greenland, the ships had to be continually at sea, but in addition, whaling in Davis Strait was more dangerous because of the icebergs and drift ice.

The first whalers there were working in a completely unknown environment. Ships' captains had to be extremely careful and unusually skilful if they were to avoid becoming trapped by the ice and losing both ships and crews. The profit margin was higher, but the cost of outfitting was greater and the journey was two months longer than the journey to Spitsbergen so the ships had to leave in early March.

The English returned to the whale hunt when the Davis Strait whale stocks were discovered. While it is not possible to say in precisely which year the English first came to Davis Strait, it appears clear that the discovery did in fact provide them with a strong incentive to renew their whaling effort. The English attitude to whaling was also changed by Henry Elking's *View of the Greenland Trade and Whale-fishery*, written in 1722. Around 1720 England had no involvement in the whale hunt because of its past failures, and many people concluded from the Spitsbergen episode that England could not compete with Holland in this field. Elking spoke up against these arguments in his 1722 book:

> It is a vulgar Error, but so riveted in the Minds of ignorant People, that it will be very hard to persuade them to the contrary that the Dutch can fit out their Ships, and go to Greenland, and in a word, carry on the Whale-Fishery cheaper and to more Advantage than the English.[24]

It is true that the Dutch ships cost less to build, but then the English ships were built better, lasted longer, and required fewer repairs. Crews available to the English were just as skilled and less costly, and the cost of the journey and of outfitting were less as well .

In 1725, either as a result of Elking's recommendations or as a result of the increased value of oil, which was in high demand, the South Sea Company, founded in 1711, outfitted 12 300-ton ships.[25] The harpooners were foreigners, and a good many of the crew were from the Orkneys or Shetlands, as was much of the gear. All products imported from Greenland or the Davis Strait by the company were duty-free on condition that they enter England on British ships at least a third of whose crew members were British subjects. However, the company made the same mistake as the Muscovy Company in that it paid some of the crew members fixed wages, and these men were therefore less motivated. Between 1725 and 1733, when the company stopped whaling, it lost £177,782.[26] Such a loss seems inconceivable at a time when a ship that brought back three whales could expect a profit, and when one good season would generally make up for six bad ones. Around the same time — between 1699 and 1708 — the Dutch outfitted 1652 ships and took 8537 whales, the products of which were sold for 26,385,120 florins, with a net profit of 4,727,120 florins, or £393,926.[27]

In 1733 England began to subsidize whaling operations. The amount was 20 shillings per ton for all ships over 200 tons.[28] This produced few results, except that it encouraged English merchants to outfit ships to bring back to England oil produced by New England whalers, effectively lowering the customs duties by 50 per cent.[29] An increase in the bounty to 30 shillings in 1740 also failed to put the industry back on its feet. Only when the bounty was increased to 40 shillings in 1749 did the industry revive. The number of English whaling ships in Davis Strait rose from two in 1749 to 20 in 1750. With Scottish ships appearing on the scene as well, the number rose to 40 in 1752, 49 in 1753, 67 in 1754, 82 in 1755 and 83 in 1756.[30]

The bounties were not the only reason for the revival. There was also an increased demand for oil, mainly from the textile industry, which used it to wash wool before spinning. Although whale oil did have a reputation for high quality, it was the low price that gave it the edge over rapeseed oil. Given the great demand for military uniforms during the second half of the 18th century, whale oil had a guaranteed market. Industrialization and urbanization also increased demand as the oil was used for lighting and in paints and lubricants.

The English whaling effort increased even more with the onset of the American War of Independence. The war deprived England of a large amount of oil; before the 1770s no less than 90 per cent of whale oil entering England had been produced by New England whalers.[31] England thus had no choice but to produce its own oil. In order to do this, and also to train new sailors for British warships, Parliament decided in 1775 on a tax exemption for ships going whaling in the Gulf of St. Lawrence, or to Newfoundland and Labrador. This applied to all British-built ships of 50 tons or more if the crew had at least 15 men of whom three-quarters were British subjects. In addition, there would be bonuses of £500, £400, £300, £200 and £100 for the five biggest cargos.[32]

In 1786 England outfitted 162 ships for Greenland and Davis Strait. The figure rose to 250 in 1787 and 255 in 1788, one of which was a ship of 987 tons. Each year the government paid out almost £100,000 in bounties to 6000 whalers.[33] Between 1750 and 1788 England outfitted 1449 whaling ships headed for Greenland and Davis Strait, and Scotland outfitted 430.[34] Conditions were especially favourable because the Dutch industry was starting to go into a serious decline at this time.

In the 1790s the industry was so well established that the government was able to reduce the bounty to 25 and then to 20 shillings without halting growth. This was also the period when the English began whaling in the southern oceans. Often the ships would leave port with crews of "undesirables" who would be left on the islands, and the holds would be filled with oil for the return journey. The first expeditions went after sperm whales, which have a very regular migratory pattern. Then gradually they started to hunt right whales as well, in the bays of Tasmania, Australia and New Zealand.

English whaling was severely affected by the numerous wars of the late 18th and early 19th centuries. Whereas Great Britain outfitted 255 ships for the Arctic in 1788, only 50 were outfitted in 1800. When peace came in 1802, the number climbed to 118, but it declined again when war returned in 1803.[35] Despite the smaller number of ships, however, the amount of oil taken increased: in 1790, 97 ships brought back 3309 tons, whereas in 1804, 84 ships brought back 7053 tons.[36]

In the first decade of the 19th century the value of oil increased slightly but the value of whalebone dropped sharply, apparently as a result of a change in fashion. On the other hand, the price drop meant that whalebone could be used in a greater variety of products, and consequently prices rose again a few years later.

In sum, English whaling between 1790 and 1815 had to contend with wars and price instability. Its activities were now equally divided between the southern seas and the Pacific on the one hand and the Arctic on the other. Both locations had their advantages and disadvantages: the spermaceti obtained from the sperm whales of the warmer oceans was worth three to four times the oil obtained from the right whales, and the risk of losing ships was much greater in the Arctic, because of the ice; on the other hand, an expedition to the south took four years, the cost of outfitting was much greater, sperm whales have no baleen plates, and they give ten times less oil.

In 1816, after several unfruitful years of whaling in the southern seas and the Pacific, the British returned in force to the Arctic, outfitting 146 ships.[37] At this time, large quantities of whales were found off the west coast of Baffin Island. In 1820 the city of Hull alone sent to the Arctic 60 whaling ships, which brought back goods worth a record ₤318,000.[38]

During this period, English whaling was dominated by the Scoresbys, father and son, who did much to spread knowledge on the subject. William Scoresby Senior, born in 1760, made his first whaling trip on the *Henrietta*. In 1787 he was a harpooner; from 1791 to 1823 he captained several whaling ships, including the *Henrietta*, the *Dundee*, the *Resolution*, the *John* and the *Fame*. He died in 1829. His son (1789-1857) made his first trip at the age of ten with his father, on board the *Dundee*. He took courses in chemistry and geography in 1807 and 1808, and was appointed commander of the *Resolution* in 1810 and of the *Esk* in 1813. He was made a member of the Royal Society of Edinborough in 1819 and a fellow of the Royal Society of London in 1824. He wrote numerous scientific works, including *An Account of the Arctic Regions with a History and Description of the Northern Whale-fishery*, which appeared in 1820. The first volume of this masterpiece deals with Arctic geography, hydrography, ice, climate and fauna. The second is wholly devoted to whaling in the Arctic — and specifically whaling by the English. It was written during the golden age of English whaling in Greenland and Davis Strait, the author having been a participant in many of the yearly trips. Because Scoresby had a keen sense of observation and was at the forefront of scientific knowledge, he was able to write a book that is still one of the best on the subject for its accuracy, its concern for detail, and its scientific character.[39]

According to Scoresby, the ideal Arctic whaling ship was 330-340 tons.[40] A smaller ship would require just as large a crew while a bigger one would mean unnecessary expenditures. It was more expensive to outfit Arctic whalers because of the changes that had to be made in the ship's architecture. To be ice-resistant, they had to be reinforced inside with additional beams and iron-plated on the outside. They left for Greenland in March or April, and for Davis Strait in late February. No cargo was carried on the outward journey, making a good catch essential if the owners were to recover their costs. The ships first headed up the coast of Labrador, continuing north to Cumberland Sound. In May they crossed to the east side of the sound, and in July they went up to Baffin Bay, returning in early November. Pack ice was ideal for killing whales because there were few places where they could surface to breathe, but the ice was very dangerous and many ships got crushed.

The cost of outfitting was amply covered by 40-50 tons of oil. A ship that came back empty would lose ₤2000.[41] Since a single Greenland whale from Davis Strait would generally give a ton of whalebone and 21 tons of oil, one had to be very unlucky not to cover costs. A typical cargo of oil was 160 tons.[42] In 1813 the *Esk* under William Scoresby returned with a cargo of 354 tons worth ₤11,000.[43]

34

Unlike the Basques and the Americans, the English never boiled the blubber on board ship. The main reason was that the English mostly went after Greenland whales, and the ovens on board could not handle that much blubber: sperm whales yielded two tons of oil compared to 21 tons for Greenland whales. Low Arctic temperatures also made rendering operations more difficult.

The oil was used in lighting streets,[44] workshops, homes, mills and stores, in the manufacture of soft soaps, varnishes, paints and rope, and in the preparation of leather and wool. Some of it was also used as a lubricant.

The year 1820 marks the height of the English whaling industry, and the beginning of its decline. The main reasons were more frequent use of coal gas and rapeseed oil, the decrease in the number of whales, and the ending of bounties in 1824. In the 1830s many whalers diversified by going after seals as well as whales, but this lasted only a short time and it was not an effective solution. By 1844 the English whaling fleet had only 85 ships, compared to a high of 323 in the early 1820s.[45] In the second half of the 19th century the industry was on its last legs. Capitalists were no longer investing in it, and young sailors refused to sign up on whaling ships. Only the Scots continued to outfit ships for whaling: Aberdeen, Peterhead and Dundee in particular replaced Hull and London. Because of its large jute industry, Dundee flourished as a port until the early 20th century, but whaling disappeared from the Arctic.

1 Harpooning. This illustration, like Figures 2-9, shows a whaling scene based on John Monck's story of whaling in Spitsbergen in 1619-20. (Awnsham Churchill, *A Collection of Voyages and Travels* [London: Henry Lintot, 1744], Vol. 4, p. 750. Public Archives Canada, Picture Division, C-118303.)

2 Towing the whale. (Awnsham Churchill, *A Collection of Voyages and Travels* [London: Henry Lintot, 1744], Vol. 4, p. 750. Public Archives Canada, Picture Division, C-118308.)

3 Cutting the whale up. (Awnsham Churchill, *A Collection of Voyages and Travels* [London: Henry Lintot, 1744], Vol. 4, p. 750. Public Archives Canada, Picture Division, C-118304.)

4 The whaling facility on shore. (Awnsham Churchill, *A Collection of Voyages and Travels* [London: Henry Lintot, 1744], Vol. 4, p. 750. Public Archives Canada, Picture Division, C-118309.)

5 Boiling the blubber. (Awnsham Churchill, *A Collection of Voyages and Travels* [London: Henry Lintot, 1744], Vol. 4, p. 750. Public Archives Canada, Picture Division, C-118305.)

6 Coopers at work. (Awnsham Churchill, *A Collection of Voyages and Travels* [London: Henry Lintot, 1744], Vol. 4, p. 750. Public Archives Canada, Picture Division, C-118311.)

7 Preparing the baleen plates. (Awnsham Churchill, *A Collection of Voyages and Travels* [London: Henry Lintot, 1744], Vol. 4, p. 750. Public Archives Canada, Picture Division, C-118310.)

8 The whale hunt in Spitsbergen in 1630. (Awnsham Churchill, *A Collection of Voyages and Travels* [London: Henry Lintot, 1744], Vol. 1, p. 442. Public Archives Canada, Picture Division, C-118314.)

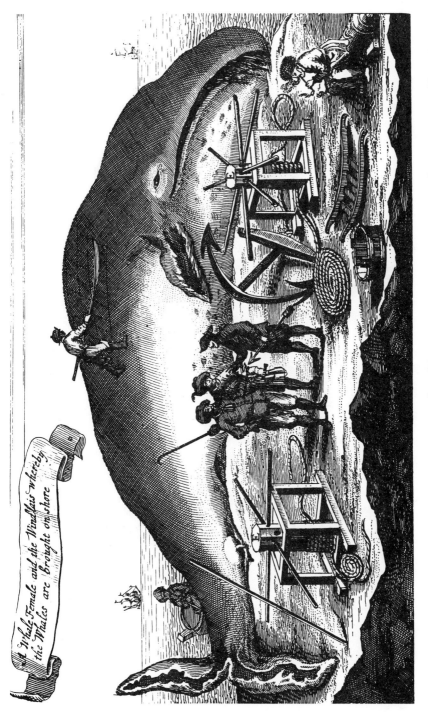

A Whale Female and the Windlass whereby the Whales are Brought on shore

9 Winches for dragging the whale onto shore. (Awnsham Churchill, *A Collection of Voyages and Travels* [London: Henry Lintot, 1744], Vol. 1, p. 444. Public Archives Canada, Picture Division, C-118313.)

10 Whalemen. 1, 2, 3: Dutch whalemen holding lances (1, 3) and a gaff (2); 4, 5, 6: Basque whalemen throwing a harpoon (4), holding one of the bayonets used to finish off wounded whales (5), and coiling a rope (6). (Sanez Antonio Reguart, *Diccionario historico de los artes de la pesca nacional* [Madrid: n.p., 1795], in Rafael Gonzalez Echegarry, *Balleneros Cantabros* [Santander: Institucion cultural de Cantabria, 1978], p. 133.)

11 Dutch whaling vessel of the 17th century. (Sanez Antonio Reguart, *Diccionario historico de los artes de la pesca nacional* [Madrid: n.p., 1795], in Rafael Gonzalez Echegarry, *Balleneros Cantabros* [Santander: Institucion cultural de Cantabria, 1978], p. 134.)

12 Dutch whalemen harpooning a whale. (Sanez Antonio Reguart, *Diccionario historico de los artes de la pesca nacional* [Madrid: n.p., 1795], in Rafael Gonzalez Echegarry, *Balleneros Cantabros* [Santander: Institucion cultural de Cantabria, 1978], p. 137.)

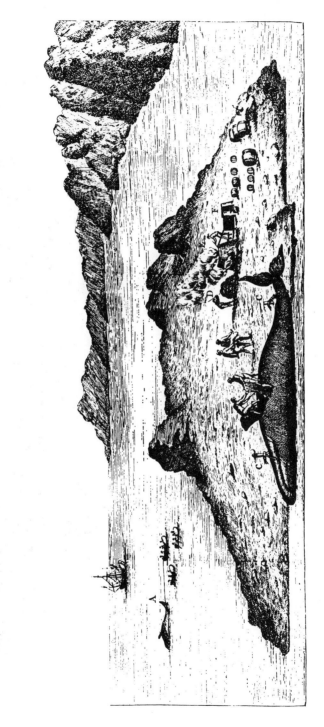

13 Cutting up a whale on land and boiling the blubber. A, whale being towed to shore; C, whale anchored to the shore and being cut up; D, pieces of blubber waiting to be boiled; E, oven; and F, vats of water to cool the oil. (Sanez Antonio Reguart, *Diccionario historico de los artes de la pesca nacional* [Madrid: n.p., 1795], in Rafael Gonzalez Echegarry, *Balleneros Cantabros* [Santander: Institucion cultural de Cantabria, 1978], p. 143.)

14 Cutting up a whale alongside a ship. (Sanez Antonio Reguart, *Diccionario historico de los artes de la pesca nacional* [Madrid: n.p., 1795], in Rafael Gonzalez Echegarry, *Balleneros Cantabros* [Santander: Institucion cultural de Cantabria, 1978], p. 144.)

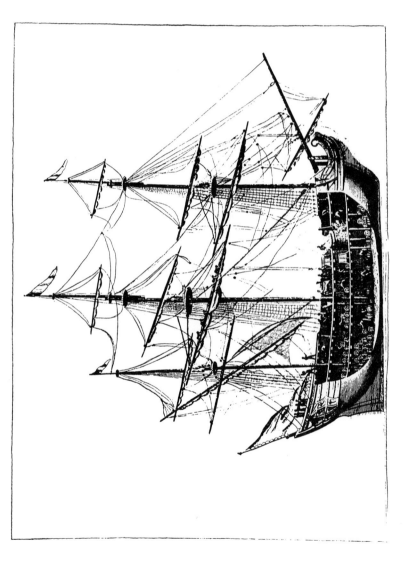

15 Storing whale oil on a ship. (Sanez Antonio Reguart, *Diccionario historico de los artes de la pesca nacional* [Madrid: n.p., 1795], in Rafael Gonzalez Echegarry, *Balleneros Cantabros* [Santander: Institucion cultural de Cantabria, 1978], p. 147.)

THE DUTCH

If the Basques were the first to make whale hunting an industry, the Dutch were the first to engage in intensive whaling. The Dutch and the English began whaling at Spitsbergen just one year apart, but for economic and political reasons, the Dutch outdistanced their competitors in a few years and remained the dominant whaling power for over a century.

The Dutch in Spitsbergen

Exploration of the polar seas to find a new passage to the Indies began in the late 16th century. During one expedition in 1596 the Dutchman William Barents, with his pilot, Jacob Heemskerke, and Captain Hendickszoon, discovered the island of Spitsbergen.

Barents lost his life, but his voyage was important because it revealed that there were large numbers of whales around the island. However, like the English, the Dutch took some years to begin exploiting these whale stocks. It was not until 1612 that they outfitted their first expedition, consisting of a single ship under Allen Sallowes, the former employee of the Muscovy Company of London mentioned earlier.[1] The following year the Dutch were able to send two ships, but these were seized by the Muscovy Company on the pretext of enforcing th exclusive whaling rights granted by King James. The Dutch estimated their losses at 130,000 guilders,[2] and resolved to avoid any repetition of the incident: as a counter to the Muscovy Company, the representatives of the chambers of commerce of several Dutch towns formed the Noordsche Company. In 1614 the company sent a fleet of 18 whalers to Spitsbergen, accompanied by four warships as protection and to demonstrate that the Dutch did not recognize King James's charter to the Muscovy Company.

In 1615, 1616 and 1617, Holland outfitted 14, 4 and 12 ships respectively for whaling in Spitsbergen.[3] In 1617 the charter of the Noordsche Company was renewed for four years. The new charter prohibited anyone from whaling in Spitsbergen without authorization; the penalty was confiscation of the offending ship and a fine of 6000 guilders.[4] During this period, the Dutch, like the English, were using Basque whalers to direct whaling operations. Also at this time Holland began whaling off the island of Jan Mayen southwest of Spitsbergen.

The rivalry between the English and the Dutch again degenerated into armed conflict in 1618. This time the Dutch were the winners. Since these conflicts benefitted no one, the various parties (Holland, England, Denmark, France, Hamburg and the Basques) finally came to an agreement on dividing up Spitsbergen among themselves. The Dutch got second choice, and took North Bay, South Bay and Holland Bay as well as little Amsterdam Island off the northwest tip of Spitsbergen. Today this island is just a rocky desert where birds nest, but in the 17th century it was the location of Smeerenberg, founded in 1619. Smeerenberg means "melting city," a term that perfectly described the place as it was in the 1620s and 1630s. Dozens of ships were anchored along the shores, others continually arriving or departing. The town included inns, taverns, shops, a fort and even a church. The 12,000 to 18,000 whalers who populated Smeerenberg were served by a number of merchants and tradesmen, including bakers, and blacksmiths who made harpoons and spears.[5] According to a chronicler of the time named Martens, the men lived in immense tents measuring 24 by 15 metres:

> The front door opened on a great room, in which were the men's sleeping-bunks. A wall with a door in it opened thence into a smaller room behind call "the buttry".... The back door opened on this smaller room, and from it went a staircase to the loft or attic.... The coopers' worksheds, with an attic for the men to sleep in, were separate buildings, and so were the warehouses. There were also many smaller huts.[6]

There were huge warehouses all around the island, and mountains of casks. The ovens operated day and night, and the oil accumulated so rapidly that ships were assigned solely for the purpose of transporting oil to Holland.

There exist six accounts of Dutch whaling expeditions to Spitsbergen during this period, as well as a history written by Zorgdrager in 1720, according to whom:

> The ships anchored in Dutch Bay, off the flat of Smeerenberg, in a row one behind another, or so near to one another that a sloop could just pass between to tow the oil-casks from ashore on board. An anchor was let go from forward into the bay and the ship made fast astern with a rope to the shore, either to the foundations of the kettles (coppers), or to some large stone, or to the jawbone of a whale, whereof some are still to be seen in various places as high piles set up for the purpose on the beach. Lying here, as in a desired and safe haven, three or four miles inland from the sea, preserved and protected from all winds, they pursued their fishery with convenience and enjoyment, rowing their sloops round and to the ships in the bay, which in those days was generally full of fish, as their doings and remains sufficiently manifest in various accounts of this fishery, otherwise they would not have settled themselves so solidly by their oil cookeries and laid up their ships so comfortably at anchor. Besides, they brought up double crews of sixty, seventy, and even eighty men, which were apportioned some to the sloops to kill the fish and tow them to the oil cookeries on the shore, others to remain on land and cut up the blubber from the fish, chop it up small, boil down to oil, fill it into casks, and roll them down to the water. Others again were on the ships to bring

the casks along-side, hoist them aloft with a pulley, and lade them into the ship.[7]

Each city that was a member of the Noordsche Company had its own shore establishment, with a winch to hoist the whales onto shore, pull the ships to anchor, and lift the blubber and the oil casks. According to one writer, the use of these winches, connected to slides, was one of the three Dutch contributions to whaling, the other two being the establishment of seasonal bases like Smeerenberg, and military protection for the whaling fleet.[8] Each Dutch town also had its own oil-rendering facility, the best locations along the shore being taken by the older and better-represented places such as Amsterdam, Rotterdam and Hoorn. All equipment for the shore stations was transported to Spitsbergen by ships specially assigned to that task. Some of the equipment, including the whaleboats, was left there for the next season.[9] Each ship was headed by two men: a captain in charge of navigating, and a *specksynder* or *specksioneer* in charge of the whaling operation itself. The *specksioneer* was almost always Basque; with time and experience, his job was taken over by the captain.

The founding of Smeerenberg, coupled with the many problems being experienced by the English, catapulted Holland into the position of leading whaling power in the early 1620s. During the first three decades of Dutch activity they did their whaling in the bays of Spitsbergen, and specifically at Smeerenberg. When the Dutch prohibited whaling by the Basques at Smeerenberg, the latter destroyed the Dutch station on the island of Jan Mayen in 1632. To minimize the risk of a fresh attack, the Dutch tried leaving some of their whalers on Jan Mayen over the winter, but the harsh climate drove them away.

By the late 1630s whales were already becoming more scarce in the bays of Spitsbergen. They were taking refuge from the hunt on the high seas, forcing the whalers to follow them and thus making the shore stations useless. Thus around 1640 whaling activity at Smeerenberg ceased. Thereafter it served only as a stopping-off spot or rescue station. The Noordsche Company disappeared when the whalers left Spitsbergen, resulting in the end of exclusive whaling rights; this in turn freed trade and reinvigorated the Dutch effort. The liberalization after 1645 was closely tied to the swift rise of the Dutch industry in the second half of the 17th century. Whereas the Noordsche Company had outfitted only a few dozen ships before 1642, in the 1670s the Dutch fleet increased to 300 ships and 18,000 whalers.[10]

The Dutch whalers hunted at that time in the bays of Spitsbergen, off Norway to the east, and off what is now Greenland to the west. Each ship had to deposit 6000 guilders as a guarantee that it would return with its cargo.[11] In this way the Dutch government ensured that it would have exclusive control of the whale-products trade. The 1670s marked the beginning of the peak period of Dutch whaling. From 1675 to 1721 the Dutch outfitted 6884 ships and killed 32,908 whales, for a total value of 150 million florins, or £14 million sterling.[12] In the 1680s the Dutch fleet made up 70 per cent of all whaling ships in the world.[13] Between 1699 and 1708 alone, the Dutch outfitted 1652 ships and took 8537 whales for a total value of 26,385,120 florins and a net profit of

4,727,120 florins.[14]   The record year, however, appears to have been 1680, when 260 ships went out with 14,000 whalers.[15]   The Basques and the English had practically abandoned whaling by this time, leaving the field open to the Dutch, who now supplied all Europe with oil and whalebone.   Nationally the whale trade was even more lucrative than the spice trade for which Holland is famous: the Dutch had to pay out florins in exchange for the spices, but the whale trade involved no exodus of money at all; to the contrary, it brought foreign money in.   A further advantage of whaling was that the products were not perishable.[16]

When whaling activity moved from the bays of Spitsbergen to the high seas, hunting and processing techniques had to be modified.   Since the shore was too far off, the whales could not be taken to the ovens to boil the blubber.   The Dutch could have copied the Basques and brought the ovens to the whales, processing the blubber on board ship.   But they always refused to do this for fear of fire.   They preferred to cut the blubber into chunks and store it in large casks for boiling in Holland.   The disadvantage of this was that less oil was produced, and of lower quality.[17]

To the Dutch the ideal whaling ship at this time was a 400-tonner measuring 33.5 by by 8.7 by 3.6 metres,[18] reinforced with metal plates, and carrying a crew of 40 to 50.   It would have three masts and a steeply inclined bowsprit.   The deck would be relatively open, and the forecastle, though above decks, would be below the rail.   The Dutch had a preference for fore-and-aft sails, which permitted better manoeuvring in ice and in fjords.   Breakfast for the crew was gruel; the other meals consisted of marinated meat, dried fish, peas and bread with water. When possible, the crew ate fresh fish, eggs or plants they found on the coast.   They thus avoided illnesses that come from poorly balanced diets.[19]

Once they had caught and cut up a whale, they packed the chunks of blubber in casks the French called *quartaux*, the Germans *kartels*, the English *quardeels* and the Dutch themselves *kardeels*.   These casks held 64 English gallons.[20]   Inside them the volume of the blubber would decrease 20 per cent because of fermentation.   Once back in Holland, the contents would be emptied into a large vat and stirred to give a more liquid consistency.   Then the fires would be lighted and the blubber poured into a wide, flat copper kettle inside a brick and masonry framework.   The kettle would hold two *kardeels* of blubber.   Once the blubber was hot, it was stirred to separate the portions that would not melt.   As the oil accumulated in the kettle, it was collected with ladles and put in the first of three small vats.   This first vat was higher than the second, and the second was higher than the third, and they were joined by a gutter.   Each of them contained water to cool the oil.   Once the first vat was full, the oil would flow into the second, and then into the third.   As it left the third vat it was sufficiently cool and clear to be put in barrels and thence it would go to market in Holland or abroad.[21] According to Duhamel du Monceau, oil produced in this way was sold at a lower price because it had a smell as a result of the blubber sitting in the casks.[22]

The Dutch in Davis Strait

The Dutch were the first to hunt whales in Davis Strait, beginning in 1719. Two years later they had a fleet of 251 ships working either in the strait or in Greenland.[23] In 1725 a French document on whaling and outfitting at Saint-Jean-de-Luz speaks of 400 Dutch ships and 20,000 sailors — 20 times the size of the French fleet.[24] Outfitting the Dutch fleet cost 1,800,000 guilders, the equivalent of 18 tons of gold. Of this, 540,000 guilders was for provisions and equipment and 1,200,000 was the captains' and crews' wages. The fleet brought back 44,000 casks of blubber and 54,000 kilograms of whalebone, with a total value of 2,100,000 guilders. Subtracting handling and processing costs left gross revenues of 1,900,000 guilders. About 70 per cent of the whale products were sent abroad.[25] Each year the Dutch exported to France alone 7000-8000 barrels of oil.[26]

In the mid-18th century Holland was still dominant in the world whale-products market, but its position slipped rapidly, beginning in the 1770s when two rivals became serious competitors: the English were reconstituting their fleet, and the golden age of American whaling was getting underway. By the end of the century the Dutch industry was dying; in 1791 only 62 ships were outfitted.[27] The people who had dominated the whaling scene for a century and a half, taking 64,576 whales between 1669 and 1778, now gave way to their competitors.[28]

THE AMERICANS

The history of American whaling can be divided into three main phases: coastal whaling up to 1712, whaling on the high seas with onshore blubber processing from 1712 to 1761, and high-seas whaling with onboard processing from 1761 into the 20th century.

From 1614 to 1712

The English first settled in New England only a few years after the beginnings of the English whaling effort in Spitsbergen. It is therefore likely that the first explorers and the first settlers aleady knew something of whaling. In 1614, for instance, Captain John Smith appears to have abandoned his original exploration plans to devote himself to whaling.[1] It was also true of the crew of the *Mayflower*, a former whaling ship. Apparently they decided to settle in Cape Cod because "large whales of the best kind for oil and bone came daily alongside and played about the ship."[2] A poem by William Morrell, written in Plymouth in 1623, even suggests that the settlers were already whaling, or preparing to do so:

The mighty whale doth in these harbours lye.
Whose oyle the careful mearchant will buy.[3]

Further evidence is a royal charter of 1629, which granted whaling rights to the residents of Massachusetts.[4] And around the same time, Richard Mather declared that he had seen "mighty whales spewing up water in the air, like the smoke of a chimney, and making the sea about them white and hoary, as is said in Joab, of such incredible bigness that I will never wonder that the body of Jonas could be in the belly of a whale."[5]

The Amerindians were already whaling at this time. Captain George Waymouth described the methods they used in the account of his voyage of 1605:

One especial thing is their manner of killing the whale, which they call powdawe; and will describe his form; how he bloweth up the water; and that he is twelve fathoms long; and that they go in company of their kings with a multitude of their boats, and strike him with a bone made in fashion of a harping iron fastened to a rope, which they make great and strong of the bark of trees, which they weer out after him: then all their boats come about him, and as he riseth above water, with their arrows they shoot him to death: when they have killed him and dragged him to shore, they call all their chief lords, whom they call sagamores, divide the spoil, and give to every man a share, which pieces so distributed, they

hang up about their houses for provision: and when they boil
them, they blow off the fat, and put to their pease, maize,
and other pulse which they eat.[6]

There can be no doubt that whaling by the native population influenced
the first New England settlers. While the whites may not have learned
their whaling technique from the native people, the fact of native
whaling did encourage the settlers to imitate them.

Nevertheless, this did not happen overnight: for about 30 years,
from 1620 to mid-century, the pioneer settlers simply recovered whales
stranded on the shore or trapped in the shallow bays. At all the
settlements along the coast from the Kennebec River to Long Island
Sound revenues from such catches were divided into three equal parts:
one for the colonial government, one for the town that had jurisdiction
over the place where the whale was found, and one for the person who
made the find.[7] In 1644 the towns of Southampton and Long Island
established four lookout brigades of 11 individuals each who took turns,
two at a time, cutting up the stranded whales. These two received two
shares of the resulting income, while the other members of the brigade
received a single share. In 1645 it was decided to offer a reward of six
shillings to anyone who reported a stranded whale to a magistrate
(except on Sunday).[8]

It was around the mid-century that whaling really got underway in
New England. The first person known to have killed a whale was William
Hamilton, around 1660. As early as 1645, however, the inhabitants of
the coastal villages were outfitting whaleboats to patrol the shoreline
for one or two weeks at a time, the crews going ashore each evening to
sleep. The Indians played a big role in the hunt. They would work as
whalers or lookouts for whites, who would provide the funds. In 1650 the
inhabitants of Southampton were employing members of nearby tribes,
recompensing them with a percentage of the oil that was produced.
Evidence of this can be found in the town's account books. On 2 April
1688 Jacobus Skallenger hired Indians to hunt for whale between
1 November and 1 April, at three shillings a day each. All equipment
was to be provided by Skallenger and his associates.[9] The Indians,
principally from the Gay Head tribe, were so essential to the whaling
effort that they were exempted from a number of taxes and from
military service during the hunting period, which lasted all winter; in
addition, they could not be prosecuted during this time of year. It was
from this association between natives and whites that the American
whaling industry arose.

In the course of a few years, whaling became so important that
every man had to take his turn acting as lookout on a nearby hill. In
1684 the product of the hunt along the east coast was so great that the
governor of New York authorized a tax of ten per cent on whale oil
exported to places other than England, Jamaica, Bermuda and some
Caribbean islands.[10] In the late 1680s Secretary John Randolph declared
that "New Plimouth colony have great profit by whale killing. I believe
it will be one of our best returns, now that beaver and peltry fayle us."[11]

At the turn of the century, Nantucket became the leading whaling
port. Nantucket Island depended on whaling more than any of the other
settlements because whales were the only existing resource. The first

whale was killed there around 1660, after it had been trapped three days in the harbour — the time required to make harpoons. The islanders quickly grasped how much they stood to gain from whaling. In 1672 they brought James Lopar from Cape Cod to teach them whaling methods, and in 1690 they brought Ichabod Paddock. It was during this period that a whaler, on seeing a whale blow out at sea, is supposed to have said: "There is a green pasture where our children's grandchildren will go for bread."[12] Whaling was such a common activity among the population that the school in East Hampton closed during the whaling season. The schoolteachers were even paid in whale oil.[13]

It is clear that the New England method of whaling arose from the contact between Europeans and Amerindians. The first English settlers probably arrived with only a minimum knowledge of whaling, then still a new activity in England, but also with a technology superior to that of the native peoples. The latter had been whaling for a long time, but their tools were not adequate. The settlers did not adopt native methods, but simply used the basic approach shared by Amerindians, English, Dutch and Basques. The New Englanders improved on native technology, replacing canoes with whaleboats, bone harpoons with iron harpoons, and stone tools with metal ones. One fundamental change, however, was that before the whites arrived, the natives could only retrieve the blubber from one side of the whale because they did not know how to turn the huge animals over.

In the late 17th century, the whale hunt was conducted in the following manner in New England. Poles topped with observation platforms were erected at strategic locations along the coast. Lookouts climbed up to the platforms to keep watch, and gave a shout when they saw one or more whales.[14] The hunters, who lived near enough to hear the call, would immediately put out to sea. Paul Dudley, the chief judge of Massachusetts, wrote in 1725 that the whaleboats

> are made of Cedar Clapboards, and so very light, that two Men can conveniently carry them, and yet they are twenty Feet long, and carry six Men, viz. the harpooner in the Forepart of the Boat, four Oarmen, and the Steersman. These Boats run very swift, and by reason of their lightness can be brought on and off, and so kept out of Danger.[15]

Also, since the whaleboats were pointed at both ends, they could move just as fast backwards as forwards, and thanks to their flat bottoms, they could pivot rapidly. A Nantucket law of 1694 prohibited the cutting of cedar except for the construction of whaleboats.[16]

The hunters would chase the whale, using either oars or paddles to propel the boats. Sometimes the whale would be killed by the first blow; sometimes they had to fight with it for hours before it either succumbed or escaped, which happened quite frequently. Once the whale was caught, it would be towed ashore, using either paddles or sails to power the boat. A winch was used to lift it onto the shore and to turn it so as to be able to retrieve the blubber from all sides. The winch technique was strangely similar to that of the Dutch at Spitsbergen, described in the previous chapter. The Dutch presence for a period of time at New York may have influenced the Americans, and it is probably not just by chance that whaling first evolved in this area.

Once the whale had been cut up, the blubber was placed in carts and taken to the furnaces, which were located near the dwellings.[17] The meat served no purpose and was left behind on the shore.

Whaling in Nantucket was organized co-operatively, each hunter taking a share of the revenues proportional to his investment. The natives were paid in clothing, powder, alcohol, money and sometimes oil, which was used as a means of paying for services. Though the methods were rudimentary, they were effective. In the year 1726 alone, the inhabitants of Nantucket took 86 Biscayne whales along the coast of the island.[18] Apparently they even took 11 on a single day.[19] Whaling employed 200 men during the autumn and winter months.[20]

From 1712 to 1761

In the early 18th century, stocks of humpback and Biscayne whales began to decline along the New England coast. What had happened in Spitsbergen was being repeated in North America: in order to continue whaling, the hunters had to move away from shore and pursue their quarry out at sea. Because of the geographical location of their island, the Nantucket hunters were, in 1698, the first to attempt such expeditions.[21]

It was presumably in the course of one of these expeditions, in 1712, that Christopher Hussey, a Nantucket captain, took the first sperm whale. A storm had blown him far from shore, and he attacked the animal without clearly recognizing what it was. Sperm whales had often been sighted, but no one had previously dared to attack one.

The 19th-century American biologist Charles Scammon wrote that the sperm whale produces less oil than the right whale — 25 barrels as opposed to 60[22] — but the oil is lighter and purer. In addition, there are three products of great value exclusive to the sperm whale: teeth, ambergris and spermaceti. The teeth are high-quality ivory and were used to make decorative objects. During whaling season, carving whale teeth was a favourite pastime of crew members. Many New England museums have large collections of such carvings, called scrimshaw, and they are genuine works of art. The intestines of sperm whales sometimes contain ambergris, which fetched a high price as a fixative in perfumes. It is even said that King Charles II ate his eggs with ambergris taken from sperm whales stranded on the coast.[23] The most lucrative sperm whale product was the spermaceti. There is still no satisfactory explanation for the presence of this liquid in the whale's head. Some researchers believe that by compressing it, the whale can adjust to different depths. The head contains one ton of spermaceti in the liquid state. On exposure to air, it turns into a smooth oily paste which was sold at two or three times the price of the oil. It was used as a lubricant in delicate mechanisms, though its main use was in candle-making. Candles made from it were diaphanous and gave off a clear, brilliant light. They were considered a luxury, and were very much in demand among the wealthy classes in England. Candle-making factories prospered in New England in the 18th and 19th centuries.

Captain Hussey's adventure marked the beginning of sperm whale hunting. The sperm whale did not frequent the shallow coastal waters, so it was necessary to replace the whaleboats with ships that could navigate on the high seas. The first sloops were constructed in Nantucket around 1694. By 1715 there were six of them on the island, and the sperm whale hunt was already bringing in 5000 dollars.[24] The first expeditions lasted six weeks, or until the barrels were full of blubber. The boats went as far as Newfoundland, returned with their cargo, and put out to sea again. Beginning in 1720, Nantucket exported oil to England on English ships that came to fetch it in Boston.[25] In 1726, the island had 25 sloops that mainly hunted for sperm whale. Five years later the island was producing £3200 worth of oil.[26]

As the sperm whales moved farther and farther away from the coast, bigger and bigger ships were used and expeditions lasted longer. The ships went as far afield as Davis Strait, the Bahamas, the West Indies and Africa. In spring they moved off south toward the Carolinas, the Bahamas and the West Indies. They then turned east to the Azores, Cape Verde and the west coast of Africa. In July they moved back to Nantucket and then left immediately for the Grand Banks. The ships that worked the North Atlantic left in March or April and returned around October. Ships from all ports along the Atlantic Coast, from New England to Virginia, worked one of these two routes. In all, about 500 ships were involved in the hunt either for sperm whales or right whales.[27] This type of journey would later be called "plum-pudding," to distinguish it from the 19th-century expeditions that lasted three or even four years.

The whaling industry in New England flourished in the first half of the 19th century for a variety of reasons, including the decline of the Dutch industry, the English policy of bounties,[28] the constant increase in oil prices, and industrialization and urbanization. The city of London alone had 5000 street lamps burning whale oil. Around 1745 the hunt had reached such proportions in the American colonies that exports went directly to England without passing through Boston. The governor of Massachusetts, Thomas Hutchinson, wrote that:

> The increase of the consumption of oil by lamps as well as by diverse manufacturers in Europe has been of no small encouragement to our whale-fishery. The flourishing state of the island of Nantuckett must be attributed to it. The cod and whale-fishery, being the principal source of our returns to Great Britain, are therefore not only of provincial but national attention.[29]

The rapid growth of whaling after 1712 had a considerable effect on the technology and methods used. First there were changes in the boats. The sloops, which the Americans used when they first went whaling on the high seas, were modelled on Dutch single-masted ships of the 17th century. It must be borne in mind that the Pilgrims had stayed awhile in Holland before crossing to America, and that the Dutch had had their own colony at New York for some years. These sloops, with their shallow draught, were well suited to the shallow New England harbours. They were 30- or 40-tonners measuring 12 to 15 metres in length and 4.5 metres in width. "A square-topsail was a characteristic of these fore-and-aft rigged vessels."[30] They carried two small boats, one of which was for emergencies only. In the 1730s these sloops reached 50 tons.[31] There was no need to return to shore after each catch, and the journeys now lasted six months, during which time the crews had to be lodged and fed and the blubber had to be stored. So little by little the sloops became whaling vessels some of which, according to Obed Macy, reached 100 tons in the 1750s.[32]

Crews consisted of about 13, recruited mainly from New England ports. At Nantucket there was a lodge of female freemasons whose members refused to marry any man who had never killed a whale.[33] A whaler's apprenticeship began at age 12, and there were several stages he had to pass through. Expeditions were often of a family nature, with the captain commanding his own children, or those of his neighbours.

Since the cargoes of blubber were now much bigger, they could no longer be boiled near the whalemen's dwellings. The ovens moved down to the ports, near the unloading docks.

The changes in equipment and methods in the first half of the 19th century applied to both sperm-whale and right-whale hunting. The same ship would often be involved in both.

From 1761 to 1860

In the early 1760s American whaling underwent profound changes as ovens for boiling the blubber made their appearance on board ships. This was not new, since the Basques had already introduced the practice, but it had been forgotten during the period of Dutch and English whaling in Greenland. For practical reasons, and for safety, the Dutch and English had never boiled blubber on board their ships. The first American ship to do so was the *Betsey* from Dartmouth. The ship's log for 3 September 1762 contains the entry "knocked down try-works" (i.e. ovens).[34]

Until this time, only ships that worked the Arctic were able to preserve the blubber properly, thanks to the cold climate. Ships working in temperate regions had to return to port several times during the season. Now that blubber could be boiled on board, ships could be outfitted for three- or four-year expeditions, or until the holds were full. It was also no longer necessary to go into the dangerous Arctic waters, and the Americans stopped going there in the second half of the 18th century. Instead they went either to the Grand Banks of Newfoundland or the warm waters of the West Indies, Africa and South America.

With the ceding of Canada to England, the Gulf of St. Lawrence opened up to the Americans.[35] In 1761 they sent ten ships; in 1762, fifty; and in 1763, eighty.[36] The *News-Letter* of Boston dated 8 August 1765 reported that:

Tuesday one of the sloops which has been on the Whaling

Business returned here. We hear that the Vessels employed in the Whale Fishery from this and the neighbouring Maritime Towns, amounting to near 100 Sail, have been very successful this Season in the Gulph of Saint Lawrence and Streights of Belle Isle; having, tis said already made upwards of 9000 Barrels of Oil.[37]

That same year, however, a memorandum dated 21 July by the lieutenant governor of Newfoundland, Otto Hamilton, poured some cold water on American enthusiasm:

MEMORANDUM: In Pursuance of the Governor's Directions, all masters of Whaling Vessels, and others whom it may concern, are hereby most strictly required to observe the following Particulars, viz:

1. To carry the useless Parts of such Whales as they may catch to at least Three Leagues from the Shore, to prevent the Damage that the neighbouring Fishers for Cod and Seal sustain by their being left on the Shore.

2. Not to carry any Passengers from Newfoundland or the Labradore Coast to any Part of the Plantations.

3. To leave the Coast by the first of November at farthest.

4. Not to fish in any of the Ports or Coasts of Newfoundland lying between Point Richi and Cape Bonavista.

5. Not to carry on any Trade or have any Intercourse with the French on any Pretence.

6. In all your Dealings with the Indians, to treat them with the greatest Civility: observing not to Impose on their Ignorance, or to take Advantage of their Necessities. You are also on no Account to serve them with spirituous Liquors.

7. Not to fish for any other than Whale on this Coast.

Dated on board His Majesty's sloop Zephyr, at the Isle of Bois, on the Labradore Coast, the 21st July, 1765.[38]

Point 7 was particularly bad for the Americans since they had sometimes been able to make up for a disappointing whale hunt by fishing for cod.

The following year Governor Palliser issued the following proclamation:

By His Excellency Hugh Palliser, Governor and Commander in Chief in and over the Island of Newfoundland, the Coast of Labradore and all the Territories dependent thereupon:

Whereas a great many Vessels from His Majesty's Plantations employed in the Whale-Fishery resort to the Part of the Gulph of St. Lawrence and the Coast of Labradore which is within this Government, and as I have been informed that some Apprehensions have arisen amongst them that by the Regulations made by me relating to the different Fisheries in those Parts, they are wholly precluded from that Coast:

Notice is hereby given, That the King's Officers stationed in those Parts have always had my Orders to protect, assist and encourage by every Means in their Power, all Vessels from the Plantations employed in the Whale-Fishery, coming within this Government; and, pursuant to his Majesty's Orders to me, all Vessels from the Plantations will be admitted to that Coast on the same Footing as they have ever been admitted in Newfoundland; the ancient Practices and Customs established in Newfoundland respecting the Cod Fishery, under the Act of Parliament passed in the 10 and 11th Years of William IIId commonly called The Fishing Act, always to be observed.

And by my Regulations for the Encouragement of the Whale Fishers, they are also under certain necessary Restrictions therein prescribed, permitted to land and cut up their Whales in Labradore; this is a Liberty that has never been allowed them in Newfoundland, because of the Danger of prejudicing the Cod-Fishery carried on by our adventurers' Ships, and by Boat-Keepers from Britain, lawfully qualified with Fishing-Certificates according to the aforementioned Act, who are fitted out at a very great Risque and Expense in complying with said Act, therefore they must not be liable to have their Voyages overthrown, or rendered precarious by any Means, or by any other Vessels whatever. And

Whereas great Numbers of the Whaling Crews arriving from the Plantations on the Coast of Labradore early in the Spring considering it as a lawless Country are guilty of all Sorts of Outrages before the Arrival of the King's Ships, plundering whoever they find on the Coast too weak to resist them, obstructing our Ship Adventurers from Britain by sundry Ways, banking amongst their Boats along the Coast, which ruins the Coast-Fishery, and is contrary to the most ancient and most strictly observed Rule of the Fishery, and must not be suffered on any Account; also by destroying their Fishing-Works on Shore, stealing their Boats, Tackle and Utensils, firing the Woods all along the Coast, and hunting for and plundering, taking away or murdering the poor Indian Natives of the Country; by these Violences, Barbarities, and other notorious Crimes and Enormities, that Coast is in the utmost Confusion, and with Respect to the Indians is kept in a State of War.

For preventing these Practices in future Notice is hereby given, That the King's Officers stationed in those Parts, are authorized and strictly directed, to apprehend all such Offenders within this Government, and to bring them to me to be tried for the same at the General Assizes at this Place: And for the better Government of that Country, for regulating the Fisheries, and for protecting His Majesty's Subjects from Insults from the Indians, I have His Majesty's Commands to erect Block Houses, and establish Guards along that Coast.

This Notification is to be put in the Harbours in Labradore, within my Government, and through the Favour of His Excellency Governour Bernard, Copies thereof will be put up in the Ports within the Province of Massachusetts, where the Whalers mostly belong, for their Information before the next Fishing Season.

Given under my Hand at St. John's in Newfoundland, this First Day of August, 1766.[39]

The changes to point 1 of Lieutenant Governor Hamilton's memorandum suggest that the fishery was proving profitable to the Labrador authorities and that they had an interest in keeping the Americans away, but the Americans were now more often choosing to go to the southern seas in pursuit of the sperm whale.

In 1768 the New Englanders began exporting their whale products to the Mediterranean countries. By 1770 they were sending 6892 kilograms of spermaceti candles to Great Britain and Ireland, 6375 kilograms to other European countries, and 158,231 kilograms to the West Indies. The total value of the catch at Nantucket alone was worth £150,000.[40] The most intense whaling was carried on in the state of Massachusetts. In 1774 New England had 360 whaling vessels with a total tonnage of 33,000, employing 4700 mariners.[41] The whaling effort was producing 45,000 barrels of spermaceti, 8500 barrels of oil and 33,750 kilograms of whalebone.[42]

The American Revolution, which began in 1775, temporarily halted whaling activity. All whaling vessels were required either to remain in port or to raid enemy commerce. Whaling crews captured by the English had a choice of serving on English warships or on English whaling vessels. Most chose the latter. It was, in fact, two whaling vessels that carried the famous tea into the port of Boston.

The only whalers to continue activities during the war were those of Nantucket. It was their only source of income, and they lost no time declaring themselves neutral in the conflict so as to protect their livelihoods. At first neither England nor Congress recognized this, and the island's whalers were attacked by both sides.[43] During these years Nantucket lost 134 ships, and 1200 whalers were killed, conscripted or imprisoned. When peace came in 1783, there were 202 widows among the approximately 800 families on the island.

The Nantucket whalers were also the most affected by the peace. Americans had been deprived of whale products during the war and had become accustomed to substitutes, which they then continued to use after the war ended. In addition, England imposed a heavy duty of £18 on every ton of spermaceti imported from the United States. Nantucket thus lost its markets. Many of the biggest whalers could not survive, and left to settle in Nova Scotia or even in France, where they outfitted six whaling vessels for Louis XVI.

In 1789 the industry recovered, thanks to a trading agreement between France and the United States. Some merchants continued to export their products to England despite the heavy tax. Indeed, the first American ship to drop anchor at the Tower of London after the Treaty of Versailles was the whaling vessel *Bedford* bringing a cargo of oil. But the English market was restricted, and the agreement with France opened a new and very profitable market for the Americans. In the United States itself the use of spermaceti became more and more fashionable. The American government used it for its many lighthouses.

Around the same time, the whaling grounds of the Pacific Ocean were opening up. The first whaling vessel to round Cape Horn was the *Amelia*, owned by Charles Enderby of London, in 1788. The American ship *Beaver* did the same in 1791. The struggle for control of whaling in the Pacific had begun, involving France, England and the United States, and it was to continue into the 20th century. The rivals fought it out on the seven seas; thousands of men and ships, and millions in capital were involved. Eventual American supremacy in the Pacific was a great factor in the rapid rise of the United States as a world power.

The maritime wars of the late 18th and early 19th centuries boosted the American whaling effort by freeing it of its competitors. The industry was already showing promising signs in the early 19th century. In 1807 Nantucket was still the most important American whaling port and had 120 ships working off Brazil and the Cape of Good Hope, in the Pacific and even Australian waters.[44] The War of 1812, like the War of Independence, put a temporary brake on these developments: many ships were captured by the British and by Chilean and Peruvian pirates. Nantucket began the war with 116 ships and ended it, in 1815, with only 23.[45]

With the signing of peace in 1815, the golden age of American whaling began: a half-century of intense activity recorded by such historians as Obed Macy and, more recently, Alexander Starbuck. It was also described by fiction writers such as Herman Melville, whose masterpiece *Moby Dick* paints a broad panorama of whaling, based on research into the smallest details. To whaling historians, the novel is first and foremost the description of an expedition to hunt sperm whale; the fictional part is merely a pretext for the author to provide an accurate and detailed picture of early-19th-century whaling.

Six years after the end of the War of 1812, Nantucket already had 84 ships.[46] Beginning in the early 1820s, growth was rapid and constant. It was based on trade with the West Indies and increased demand for lighting oil. The United States enjoyed a period of great economic growth, and sperm whale oil and spermaceti candles were finding more and more buyers in the United States. In 1829 the American fleet had 203 ships; in 1834 it had 421 in 30 ports along the coast.[47] American whaling vessels ranged the Pacific as far west as Japan. Around 1842, the United States had one-third of all the whaling vessels in the world.[48] In 1844 there were 644 such vessels, with a combined tonnage of 200,484, and 17,594 whalemen. Of these vessels, 385 worth an average of 55,000 dollars each and with crews of about 28 men were hunting sperm whales, while 329 worth an average of 40,000 dollars and with crews also averaging 28 were hunting right whales.[49] The state of American whaling at this time was best described by Grinnell of New Bedford, addressing Congress in 1844:

> I have prepared with great care a table from authentic sources, to show the consumption of domestic and foreign articles by our whaling fleet, now consisting of 650 ships, barques, brigs, and schooners, tonnaging 200,000 tons; cost at the time of sailing, $20,000,000; manned by 17,500 officers and seamen, one half of whom are green hands when the vessels sail. By this table, it will be seen that the annual consumption by this fleet is $3,845,500; only $400,000 is of foreign articles. This great source of wealth to the nation is dependant mainly on a home market for its products. The

value of the annual import of oil and whalebone in a crude state is $7,000,000; when manufactured it probably is increased in value to $8,000,000 or $9,000,000. The whole amount of exports of oil, whalebone, and sperm candles is only $2,000,000; leaving $6,000,000 or $7,000,000 to be consumed in this country. The duties on each whale ship and outfits of 300 tons, amount to $1700.

This fleet of whaling ships is larger than ever pursued the business before. Commercial history furnishes no acount of any parallel; our ships now outnumber those of all other nations combined, and the proceeds of its enterprise are in proportion, and diffused to every part of our country. The voyages of those engaged in the sperm fishery average three and a half years; they search every sea, and often cruise three or four months with a man at each mast-head on the look-out, without the cheering sight of a whale. This fleet is manned by 17,500 Americans. They are hardy, honest, and patriotic, and will, as they did in the last war, stand by their country when in danger; they will man our ships, and fight our battles on the ocean. Should we ever again be compelled to resort to war to maintain our rights, they, with the other seamen of our country, will be the right arm of our defense.[50]

The fleet reached its peak two years later in 1846, with 735 ships totalling 233,189 tons[51] and worth over 21 million dollars; 70,000 people were working in the industry, and sales were 70 million dollars.[52] According to Lieutenant Charles Wilkes, "the American whaling fleet may be said to whiten the Pacific Ocean with its canvass."[53] The port of New Bedford alone had 254 ships. Its nearest rival, Nantucket, had 75.[54] Nantucket was now declining as a whaling port because its shallow channel could not admit the ever larger ships.

American whaling techniques during the first half of the 19th century are of some interest because they were to some extent similar to Basque techniques two centuries earlier. During the second half of the 18th century, the ships had begun to move away from shore, boiling the blubber on board. Around 1830 they were making expeditions that might last up to four years. By this time every sea and ocean was accessible. Some whaling vessels were even circling the globe in pursuit of their quarry. The ships ranged from 200 to 500 tons; most were 400. They were generally wide, slow and inelegant, but speed was not important; these were functional ships. They carried great quantities of blocks and other equipment including ovens, vats, tanks, whaleboats and barrels, as well as provisions to last a crew of 30 men for several months.[55] These were perhaps the most sturdy sailing ships ever built. Some operated for over 80 years; one of them, the *Truelove*, actually lasted 109 years.[56] Very few (about one per cent) were lost. There are dozens of descriptions of them in the literature:

The ships were blunt-nosed, wide-bellied craft ... made to withstand hard wear and bad weather rather than to make speed. Generally ship-rigged with three square sails, the decks flush fore and aft, masts straight as match-sticks and a jaunty bowsprit at a forty-five-degree angle, they could seldom be mistaken for anything but whalers. For if despite these distinguishing characteristics any question of their identity should still remain, it was completely given away by the four or five whaleboats always hanging from the cranes set along the bulwarks, the brick try-works for boiling the blubber built in between mainmast and foremast, and the smoke-begrimed sails and upper spars.[57]

One feature of the ships — ease of handling — was a great advantage when most of the crew were engaged in pursuit of the whale and there remained only five or six men on board.

Crews were between 30 and 40 men, depending on tonnage and the number of whaleboats aboard. Beginning in the 1830s the crews became quite cosmopolitan, including, for instance, Portuguese, and natives from the South Pacific islands. Melville immortalized the role of these native people in the character of Queequeg. The two main reasons for recruiting foreigners were the exceptional growth of the industry and the low wages, which discouraged Americans of British stock. Only 30 per cent of the revenues of whaling went to the whalers. Once this amount had been divided, unequally, among all the crew members, simple seamen received about 20 cents a day plus board. At this time, a labourer working on land earned 90 cents a day, of which 55 cents remained after deducting the cost of food and lodging — almost three times the seaman's wage.[58] Nevertheless, this did not stop men from signing on: sometimes they could not find other employment; sometimes they needed to get out of the country for some reason; many of them were carried away with visions of world travel, while others were simply taken in by the fine promises made by ships' outfitters, who posted notices such as the following:

LANDSMEN WANTED

One thousand stout young men, Americans, wanted for the fleet of whaleships, now fitting out for the North and South Pacific Fisheries. Extra chances given to Coopers, Carpenters, and Blacksmiths. None but industrious young men with good recommendations taken. Such will have superior chances for advancement. Outfits, to the amount of Seventy-Five Dollars furnished to each individual before proceeding to sea. Persons desirous to avail themselves of the present splendid opportunity of seeing the world and at the same time acquiring a profitable business, will do well to make early application to the undersigned.[59]

The great majority of crew members were about 20 years old and had no experience at sea. They were trained by the captain and officers during the crossing to the whaling ground. Life on board was harsh, and punishments were severe. The smallest offences could lead to whipping and hanging by the thumbs. In 1844 the whaleman Justin Martin wrote "That it would be better ... to be painted black and sold to a southern planter than be doomed to the forecastle of a whaling ship."[60] In the 1840s the average length of an expedition was 42 months, during which time the crew never went ashore except to take on supplies (in the Azores and Cape Verde, for instance). The ship was home for these men of the sea. Perhaps the most striking case is that of an American whaler who, in 11 years of marriage, had spent only 360 days with his wife.[61]

When everything on board was ready for the hunt, but there were no whales, boredom would set in. There were a few diversions — dancing, dice, cards, dominos, carving — but these were not always sufficient to fill up the many slack periods and to make men forget how long they had been away from home. Dulles gives the example of a ship that was at sea for 1450 days and put its boats into the water only 175 times, to take 57 animals.[62] Allowing for time spent cutting them up and boiling the blubber, the crew would still have had 700 days with nothing to do. An entry in the log of the *California* expresses the feelings of the idle crew: "Fine weather, weather, weather all day."[63]

When the lookout at the top of the mast cried "Thar she blows," the crew would suddenly come to life. Since sperm whales are gregarious, a sighting of one or two would mean that a school was present, and all the boats would be put in the water in hopes of catching as many as possible. The boats were suspended from metal or wood davits, three on the port side and on to starboard. They were 8.4 to 9 metres long, 1.8 metres wide, 55 centimetres deep in the middle and 92.5 centimetres deep at the two ends:

> It is sharp at both ends, with flaring sides, and is of a model that insures great swiftness, as well as the qualities of an excellent sea-boat. At the bow (or "head," as whalers usually term it) is a groove, in which is placed a metal sheave, over which the line runs; near the end and upper edges of the groove, a slender pin, of tough wood or whalebone, passes across through holes above the line, to prevent it from flying out when running. This groove is called the "chocks." About three feet from the stern is the "clumsy-cleet," a stout thwart with a rounded notch on the after side, in which the officer or boat-steerer braces himself by one leg against the violent motion of the boat, caused by a rough sea, or the efforts of the whale while being "worked upon." The space between the clumsy-cleet and the chocks is covered with a sort of deck, six inches below the gunwales, and is called the "box," or "box of the boat." Five thwarts, or seats, for the accommodation of the rowers, are placed at proper distances apart, between the clumsy-cleet and stern sheets; and opposite each rowlock, near the bottom of the boat, is a well-fastened cleet, to receive the end or handle of the oar, which is called a "peak-cleet"; and when fast to a whale, or when the crew are resting, the end of the oar is placed in the hole of this cleet, while the heavy portion still rests in the rowlock, thereby elevating the blade far above the water. About four feet of the stern is decked over, through the forward part of which, a little to one side, is placed the loggerhead, shaped like a post with a large head, which projects six or eight inches above the gunwales, and by this loggerhead the line is controlled when the boat is fast to the object of pursuit.[64]

The boats were light enough to be carried by two men, and they sometimes reached speeds of 16 kilometres per hour when the oars were used. The equipment on the boats included:

> One mast and yard, or sprit, one to three sails (but usually a jib and mainsail), 5 pulling-oars, one steering-oar, 5 paddles (to propel the boat), 5 rowlocks (to confine and support the oars in their proper places when rowing), 5 harpoons, one or 2 line-tubs (into which the line is coiled), 3 hand-lances, 3 short-warps (to connect the second harpoon to the main line when a second iron is thrown into the animal), one boat-spade (for cutting the cords about the "small" of the victim, or that portion of the body which connects with the flukes, crippling it, thereby retarding its progress through the water), 3 lance-warps, one boat-warp, one boat-hatchet, 2 boat-knives (to cut the line should it get foul and endanger the boat, when fast), one boat-waif (to be used as a signal or placed in a dead whale to indicate its whereabouts), one boat-compass, one boat-hook (to hook up a whale's fin or stay lines or to hold the boat in position), one drag (for "bending on" to the line to assist in impeding the whale when running, or is fastened to the line when compelled to let it go from the boat), one grapnel (to haul up the dead animal's flukes or its head in order to cut a hole and reeve the tow-rope), one boat-keg (for carrying a supply of fresh water), one boat-bucket, one jiggin (for bailing the boat), one lantern-keg (containing flint, steel, box of tinder, lantern, candles, bread, tobacco and pipes), one boat-crotch (to rest the end of the iron or lance-pole on), one tub-oar crotch (to receive the tub-oar and raise it above the line-tub, when the boat is fast to a whale), 6 chock-pins (to keep the whale-line in the chock), a roll of canvas, a paper of tacks) to cover holes which may be staved in the boat), 2 nippers (to hold on to the line when it is swiftly running out); in all 48 articles, and at least 82 pieces.[65]

There were six men in each boat: the coxswain — the officer in charge — steered the boat with an oar 6.6 metres long; the harpooner, at the front, rowed with the others until the time came to attack; finally, each of the four oarsmen had a specific role to play during the attack. All but the coxswain had their backs to the quarry.

> After the boat was lowered into the water:
> the line is placed between the two after thwarts. The men being seated in their proper places, the line from the tub is taken aft around the logger-head, then forward over the oars, and a few fathoms of it are coiled in the box of the boat; it is then termed a "box-warp." Two harpoons are placed at the head of the boat, the staves or poles of which rest in the "boat-crotch." The end of the box-wrap is made fast to the "first iron"; the "second iron" is connected with the main line by a bowline in the end of a short-warp which is bent on to the second iron. The lances are in their places at the head of the boat, on the starboard side, the boat-spade on the side opposite; the boat-hatchet and a knife in their proper places

in the head of the boat, and the other knife ready at the stern.[66]

The boat set off using either oar or sail power and approaching the whale from behind, since whales do not have good rear vision. Once the boat was within three arm-spans of the whale, the officer would give the order for the harpooner to stand up. The harpooner would launch the first harpoon with all the strength of both arms into the whale's body near the eye. If there was time, he would then throw a second harpoon; otherwise he would throw it into the sea to avoid anyone being wounded. The purpose of the harpoon was to join the whale to the boat by a line, which entered the boat through the groove in the bow, went along the side just over the oar handles, around the loggerhead and into a tub near the last oarsman's seat where it lay coiled. It was thus taut from front to back and parallel to the keel.

The boat was then carried along at great speed over the waves as the whale fled. The Americans called this a Nantucket sleigh ride. According to Ashley, the Americans did not start attaching the end of the line to the boat until the second half of the 17th century.[67] This practice, begun by the British in the Arctic, was much more dangerous than the conventional method, but it greatly reduced the number of whales that were lost.

One the chase was underway, the harpooner and the coxswain would exchange places. This peculiarly American practice has never been explained. It was quite a daring manoeuvre: two men moving the length of a boat going at full tilt and carrying some 50 pieces of gear as well as four other men, while a line unrolled at deadly speed — so fast that it had to be splashed with water to prevent it bursting into flame. Yet the move appeared to serve no purpose. The only explanation that makes sense is that the coxswain, being the head of the crew, reserved to himself the right to deliver the *coup de grâce*.

When the whale became exhausted and slowed down, the men would pull on the line to bring themselves in close. If the boat that had harpooned the whale needed help:

> the officer in charge (of the loose boat) casts one end of his line to the officer of the fast boat. The latter bends the line to his own with a rolling hitch over the head of the boat. When the line of the fast boat is almost out - about one "fake" or so remaining in the tub - the officer tightens his hitch and lets it go. Often the hitch slips to the end of the line where it is brought up by eye-slice, and the line of the fast boat is thus attached to the line of the loose boat while the whale is running. This process may be repeated as long as more line is wanted by the addition of more boats.[68]

Once near the whale, the coxswain would stab it several times with a lance, attempting to reach a vital organ like the lungs. Generally, the whale would then swim off again, and the chase had to be repeated. After a few such chases, the whale would be completely exhausted and would stop. It would be breathing rapidly and spitting out blood through its blow-hole (the whalers called this "flurrying"). The whale's death agony would sometimes last over an hour. Finally, the animal would turn over on its back and die. To check that it really was dead, a whaler would sink a lance into its eye.

All the whaling boats would then come together in order to tow the whale to the ship, which would have moved in close to the kill. The whale would be brought up on the starboard side since the boats would be hoisted up on the port davits. With its head to the stern, the whale was attached to the ship by a chain around the tail.

The cutting up of the whale was an enormous task and just as dangerous as the actual capture. The men would balance themselves on a platform positioned above the cadaver and use large knives to hew out immense chunks of blubber called "blanket-pieces." These pieces were hoisted on board using a pulley block attached to the ship's rigging. They were cut into "horse-pieces" 37 to 45 centimetres in length and 15 to 20 centimetres in width and thickness. These were in turn cut into thin slices, but not all way through, so that the final appearance of a piece before it was plunged into a kettle was that of the pages of a book, whence the whalers' name "bible-leaves."

The pieces were then boiled to turn the blubber into oil. This was done in brick and mortar ovens installed on wooden bases on the deck, near the front hatchway between the foremast and the mainmast. The ovens had two and sometimes three openings for the 250-gallon kettles which were 3.3 metres long, 2.4 metres wide and 1.2 to 1.5 metres high, and weighed about 450 kilograms. At the front, sliding iron doors provided access to the fire-boxes. The structure was separated from the deck by a tank 30 centimetres deep that was filled with seawater, and refilled as the water evaporated. The ships always carried sand in case a fire started that might spread.

The fires were lighted with very dry wood. As the blubber melted in the kettles, the residue was removed with a skimming ladle and used to feed the fire. The process produced a terrible odour: "It smells like the left wing of the day of judgement; it is an argument for the pit."[69] The oil was poured from the kettles into a copper vat, where it cooled for 24 hours before being put in 31.5-gallon barrels. It took three days to boil the blubber and store the oil from a large sperm whale. The work would continue day and night. At the end of the voyage, the men would demolish the ovens and throw them into the sea, and the ship would return to home port with the oil from some hundred whales in its hold.

The American whaling industry continued to grow in the early 1850s. According to the London Mercantile Gazette of 22 October 1852: "The number of American ships engaged in the Southern whale-fishery alone would of themselves be nearly sufficient to man any ordinary fleet of ships-of-war which that country might require to send to sea."[70] However, in the early 1860s, growth stopped. The most often noted factor in the decline — and perhaps the most important — was the discovery of petroleum in 1859. Petroleum sold at one-fifth the price of sperm oil, resulting in a drop in the price of the latter at a time when expeditions were becoming ever more costly because the scarcity of sperm whales was forcing the ships to go ever greater distances to find their quarry. In 1790 it cost 12,000 dollars to outfit a whaling vessel for two years; in 1858 it cost 65,000 dollars for a trip of the same duration.[71] Another factor was the rise of the New England cotton industry and the opening of the American West, especially the California gold rush, which attracted manpower with better wages, opportunities for advancement, and humane working conditions. Finally, the American Civil War considerably reduced the whaling fleet: the "Stone Fleet" sunk off Charlestown and Savannah consisted of whaling vessels. During the war, the number of ships dropped 50 per cent, and the total tonnage 60 per cent.[72]

Like the Basques, the English and the Dutch before them, the Americans yielded their place to another nation. In the second half of the 19th century, Norway inaugurated the modern history of whaling with the invention of the harpoon gun.

Thus the American industry had lasted a little over two centuries, bringing fortune to many and, to some extent, economic and naval power to the United States:

> We are indebted to them for the extension of our commerce in foreign countries; for valuable additions to our stock of knowledge; for all the benefits resulting from their discoveries and researches in remote parts of the world.[73]

CONCLUSION

Few mammals have occupied as important a place as the whale in the economy of the Atlantic nations. For a thousand years whaling has supplied oil and whalebone, contributed to the growth of secondary industries, and served as a training ground for mariners. Following the isolated efforts of peoples in antiquity, the art was perfected by the Basques, the English, the Dutch and the Americans. One after another they exploited the whale stocks, which they thought to be inexhaustible. The decline of the American industry in the mid-19th century marks the end of an era.

With the appearance on the scene of the Norwegians in the 1860s, the modern history of whaling begins. Present-day whaling is based on a new technology featuring harpoon guns, steam ships and factory ships. With the invention of the harpoon gun by the Norwegian Svend Foyn, whalers no longer had to chase their quarry in boats or kill the whales with a lance. The harpoon is launched from the ship and carries a charge that explodes as it enters the animal's body. The cable linking the harpoon to the ship is strong enough to keep even rorquals afloat. Previously rorquals had never been hunted, partly because of their weight and speed, but mainly because they do not float after they die. When the harpoon gun is used in tandem with a steam ship, it becomes even more deadly since these ships can move as rapidly as their quarry. They are generally accompanied by factory ships that process catches on board at sea.

Technological progress combined with increased demand for whale products has led in the 20th century to a fresh upsurge of whaling activity, and to the massacre of several species. The price of whale oil dropped sharply after the discovery of petroleum but new applications were found for the meat and bones, which went into the manufacture of glycerine, fertilizers, paint, medications, cosmetics, soaps, margarine, animal feeds and even food for human consumption. In 1927-28, factory ships took 13,775 whales; in 1930-31 they took 40,201. In 1932 the whaling nations had to come to an agreement on limiting catches in order to prevent extinction. In December 1946, delegates of 19 countries met in Washington and established the International Whaling Commission. The commission decides on the opening and closing dates of the whaling season, prohibits the killing of females accompanied by calves, establishes minimum sizes by species, and limits the number of whales that may be taken in a single trip. The commission also decides which species to protect, and designates areas where whaling is prohibited. Conformance to commission decisions is monitored on board each factory ship and at each shore station by two commission inspectors.

A modern whaling fleet includes one factory ship, 12 catcher boats, three boats to mark dead whales, two corvettes to tow the factory ship and one tank ship to carry fuel and deliver the whale products to the nearest port. A crew of 150 men can cut up a whale 30 metres long in one hour.

Although whaling is no longer as important as it was in comparison to new rising sectors of the economy, the number of catches is still very high. In their best years, the Basques never killed more than 100 whales, the Dutch, 1000 and the Americans, 5000.[1] Since the early 20th century the average annual catch has been about 20,000, with a peak of 54,835 in 1938.[2]

More than any other pursuit, whaling has demonstrated throughout history that humans have an unreasoned desire for profit. The rate of reproduction of whales is too slow to permit intensive hunting. Many species are now extinct and others are in serious danger. In the early 19th century the biologist La Cepède was already trying to make humanity aware of the danger that whales might become extinct:

> Man, attracted by the treasure that victory over the whales might afford him, has troubled the peace of their immense solitary abodes, violated their refuges, sacrificed all those which the icy unapproachable polar deserts could not screen from his blows; and the war he has made on them has been especially cruel because he has seen that it is large catches which make his commerce prosperous, his industry vital, his sailors numerous, his navigators daring, his pilots experienced, his navies strong and his power great.
>
> Thus it is that these giants among giants have fallen beneath his arms; and because his genius is immortal and his science now imperishable, because he has been able to multiply without limit the imaginings of his mind, they will not cease to be the victims of his interest until they have ceased to exist. In vain do they flee before him: his art will transport him to the ends of the earth; they will find no sanctuary except in nothingness.[3]

These thoughts are even more relevant today than they were when written.

APPENDIX A
THE ORDER CETACEA

SUBORDER MYSTICETI[1]

Family	Balaenidae			Eschrichtidae	Balaenopteridae	
Genus	Balaena	Eubalaena	Caperea	Eschrichtius	Balaenoptera[5]	Megaptera[9]
Species	Greenland whale[2]	Biscayne whale[3] southern right whale	pigmy right whale	gray whale[4]	sei whale minke whale Bryde's whale fin whale blue whale[6]	humpback whale

SUBORDER ODONTOCETI[7]

Family	Monodontidae		Delphinidae	Ziphiidae	Physeteridae		Phocoenidae
Genus	Delphinapterus	Monodon	19 genera incl. Grampus, Orcinus, Globicephala, Delphinus		Kogia (pygmy sperm whales)	Physeter	Phocoena
Species	white whale (beluga)	narwhal	grays grampus Atlantic pilot whale killer whale common dolphin	Blainville's beaked whale goose-beaked whale northern bottlenosed whale		sperm whale[8]	common porpoise

All cetaceans have horizontal caudal flukes and either one or two blowholes on top of the head.

1 The Mysticeti have baleen plates on the upper jaw.
2 Hunted in the Arctic from the 17th to 19th centuries. Has no dorsal fin and no ventral grooves. Also called bowhead whale.
3 Frequents the North Atlantic. Also called black or North Atlantic right whale. Hunted by the Basques for several centuries.
4 Has no dorsal fin but does have ventral grooves.
5 Not hunted until the late 19th century.
6 The biggest of the cetaceans; the largest animal to have ever lived.
7 The Odontoceti have teeth.
8 Hunted by the Americans. Has teeth only on the lower jaw.

NAMES OF WHALE SPECIES IN VARIOUS LANGUAGES

English	German	Norwegian	Dutch	French	Japanese	Russian
Greenland Right Whale	Grönlandwal	Gronlandshval	Groenlandse Walvis	Baleine franche	Hokkyoku Kujira	Grenlandskii Kit
Biscayan (N. Atlantic) Right Whale	Nordkaper	Nordkaper	Noordkaper	Baleine des Basques	Semi Kujira	Nastoiashchii Kit
Pigmy Right Whale	Zwergglattwal	Dvergretthval	Dwergwalvis	Baleine franche naine	Kosemi Kujira	
Californian Grey Whale	Grauwal	Grahval	Grijze Walvis	Baleine grise	Koku Kujira	Seryi Kit
Blue Whale	Blauwal	Blahval	Blauwe Vinvis	Rorqual bleu	Shironagasu Kujira	Sinii Kit
Fin Whale	Finnwal	Finhval	Gewone Vinvis	Rorqual commun	Nagasu Kujira	Seldianoi Kit
Sei Whale	Seiwal	Seihval	Noordse Vinvis	Rorqual de Rudolf	Iwashi Kujira	
Bryde's Whale	Brydewal	Brydehval	Bryde's Vinvis	Baleine de Bryde	Nitaci Kujira	
Little Piked (Minke) Whale	Zwergwal	Vagehval	Dwergvinvis	Petit rorqual	Koiwashi Kujira (Minku)	Malyi polosatik kit zalinov
Humpback	Buckelwal	Knolhval	Bultrug	Mégaptère	Zatô Kujira	Gorbatyi Kit
Sperm Whale	Pottwal	Spermhval	Potvis	Cachalot	Makkô Kujira	Kashalot
Pigmy Sperm Whale	Zwergpottwal	Dverg-Spermhval	Dwergpotvis	Cachalot nain	Komakkô	Karlikovyi Kashalot
Bottlenose Whale	Entenwal	Naebhval	Butskop	Hypérodon		Butylkonos
Beluga	Weisswal	Hvidfisk	Beluga	Delphinaptère blanc	Shiro Iruka	Belukha
Common Porpoise	Meerschwein	Nise	Bruinvis	Marsouin	Nezumi Iruka	Morskaya Svin'ya
Killer (Orca)	Schwertwal	Spaekhogger	Orca	Épaulard	Shachi	Kosatka
Pilot Whale	Grindwal	Grindhval	Griend	Globicéphale noir	Gondô Kujira	Grindy
Bottlenose Dolphin	Grosser Tümmler	Tumler	Tuimelaar	Souffleur	Handô Iruka	Afaliny
Common Dolphin	Delphin	Delphin	Dolfijn	Dauphin	Ma Iruka	Del'finybelobochka

E.J. Slijper, Whales (London, Hutchinson, 1962), p. 490.

APPENDIX C
THE EIGHT SPECIES OF WHALES KNOWN TO THE ENGLISH IN 1611

[1]   The first sorts of whales is called the bearded whale, which is black in colour, with a smooth skin, and white under the chops; which whale is the best of all the sorts; and the elder it is the more it doth yielde. This sort of whale doth yielde usually 400 to 500 fines and between 100 to 120 hogsheads of oyle.

[2]   The second sort of whale is called Sarda, of the same colour and fashion as the former, but somewhat lesse, and the fines not above one fathom long, and yeeldth in oyle according to his bigness, sometimes eightie, sometimes a hundred hogsheads.

[3]   The third sort of whale is called Trumpa, being as long as the first but not so thicke, of colour gray, having but one trunke in his head, whereas the former have two. He hath in his mouth teeth of a span long and as thicke as a man's wrist, but no finnes; whose head is bigger than either of the two former, and in proportion far bigger than his body. In the head of this whale is the spermacetti, which you are to keepe in caske apart from your other oyle; you may put the oyle you find in the head, and the spermacetti, all together and mark it from the other oyle, and at your coming home we will separate the oil from the spermacetti. The like is to be done with the oyle of this sort of whale which is to be kept apart from the oyle of the other whales. The reason is that the oyle of this sort of whale being boyled will be as white and hard as tallow; which to be mingled with the other oyle being liquid would make the same to show as footie oyle and so consequently spoyle both and be of little value; you are therefore to be very careful to keepe the oyle of this sort of whale apart as well of the head as of the body for the reasons before mentioned. In this sort of whale is likewise found the Ambergreese lying in the entrals and guts of the same, being of shape and colour like unto cowe's dung. We would have you therefore yourself to be present at the opening of this sort of whale and cause the residue of the said entrals to be put into small caske and bring them with you into England....
    The teeth likewise of this sort of whale we would have you cause to be reserved for a triall; as also any other matter extraordinarie that you shall observe in the same. This whale is said to yeelde in oyle fortie hogs' heads besides the spermacetti.

[4]   The fourth sort of whale is called Otta Sotta, and is of the same colour as the Trumpa, having finnes in his mouth all white but not above halfe a yard long, being thicker than the Trumpa but not so long. He yeeldes the best oyle but not above 30 hogs' heads.

[5]   The fifth sort of whale is called Gibarta, of colour blacke like the two first, saving that it hath standing upon the top of its back a finne halfe a yard long. This whale is as big as the first; his finnes little or nothing worth, being not above halfe a yard long, and he yeeldth about 12

hogs' heads of oyle, all of which his backe yeeldes, as for his bellie it yeeldes nothing at all.

[6]   The sixth sort is called Sedeva, being of a whitly colour and bigger than any of the former.   The finnes not above one foot long and he yeeldes little or no oyle.

[7]   The seventh is called Saveda negro; of colour blacke, with a bumpe on his backe.   This whale yeeldes neither oyle, finnes, nor teeth, and yet he is of great bignesse.

[8]   The eighth sort of whale is called Sewria, of colour as white as snow, of the bignesse of a wherrie.   He yeeldes not above one or two hogs' heads of oyle nor any finnes, and is good meat to be eaten.

Basil Lubbock, *The Arctic Whalers* (Glasgow: Brown, Son & Ferguson, 1937), p. 62.

The above list is contained in the instructions given to Thomas Edge. The species may be identified as follows: 1, Greenland whale; 2, Biscayne whale; 3, sperm whale; 4, ?; 5, some kind of rorqual; 6, blue whale?; 7, humpback whale, and 8, beluga.

EQUIPMENT AND SUPPLIES ON AN ENGLISH WHALING VESSEL IN THE 17TH CENTURY

250	hogsheds to put the bread in
150	hogsheds of cidar
6	kintals of oile
8	kintals of bacon
6	hogsheds of beefe
10	quarters of salt
150	pound of candles
8	quarters of beanes and pease saltfish & herring
4	tunnes of wines
1/2	quarter of mustard seed, and a querne
1	grindstone
800	empty shaken hogsheds
350	bundles of hoopes and 6 quintalines
800	paire of heds for the hogsheds
10	estachas called roxes for harping irons
10	pieces of arporieras
3	pieces of baibens for the javelines small
2	tackles to turne the whales
1	halser of 27 fadom long to turne ye whales
15	great javelines
18	small javelines
50	harping irons
6	machicos to cut the whale withall
2	doozen of machetos to minch the whale
2	great hookes to turne the whale
3	paire of can hookes
6	hookes for staves
3	dozen of staves for the harping irons
6	pullies to turne the whale with
10	great baskets
10	lampes of iron to carie light
5	kettles of 150 li. the piece and 6 ladles
1000	of nailes of the pinnases
500	of nailes of carabelie for the houses and the wharfe
18	axes and hatchets to cleave wood
12	pieces of lines, and 6 dozen of hookes
2	beetles of rosemarie
4	dozen of oares for the pinnases
6	lanternes
500	of Tesia
	gunpouder & matches for harqubushes
5	pinnases

4   furnaces to melt the whale in
6   ladles of copper
3   paires of bootes great and strong
8   calve skins to make aprons or barbecans

Charles Boardman Hawes, *Whaling* (London: W. Heinemann, 1924), pp. 339-341.

APPENDIX E
ENGLISH WHALING TECHNIQUE AT SPITSBERGEN

Fotherby's journal of 1613 gives us a good idea of the whaling technique used by the English at Spitsbergen. It drew heavily on Basque technique:

When the whale enters into the sounds our whale-killers doe presentlie sallie forth to meet him, either from our ships, or else from some other place more convenient for that purpose, where to expect him; making very speedie way towards him with their shallops. ...Comeing neare him, they row resolutelie towards him, as though they intended to force the shallop upon him. But, so soone as they come within stroak of him, the harponier (who stands up readie, in the head of the boat) darts his harping-iron at him out of both his hands; wherewith the whale being stricken, he present-lie descends to the bottom of the water; and therefore the men in the shallop doe weire out 40, 50, or 60 fathomes of rope, yea, 100 or more, according as the depth requireth. For, upon the sockett of the harping-iron, ther is made fast a rope, which lies orderlie coiled up in the sterne of the boat, which, I saie, they doe weire forth until they perceave him to be rising againe; and then they haile in some of it, both to give him the lesse scope, and also that it may be the stronger, being shorter. For, when he riseth from the bottome, he comes not directlie up above the water, but swimmes awaie with an uncontrowled force and swiftnes; hurrying the shallop after him, with her head so close drawen downe to the water, that shee seemes ever readie to be hailed under it. When he hath thus drawen her perhaps a mile or more, – which is done in a very short time, considering her swiftnes, then will he come spowteing above the water; and the men rowe up to him, and strike him with long launces, which are made purposelie for that use. In lanceing of the whale, they strike him as neare his swimming finne, and as lowe under water as they can convenientlie, to pierce into his intralls. But, when he is wounded, he is like to wrest the launce out of the striker's hand; so that sometimes two men are faine to pluck it out, although but one man did easilie thrust it in. And nowe will he frisk and strike with his taile verie forceablie; sometimes hitting the shallop, and splitting her asunder; sometimes also maihmeing or killing some of the men. And, for that cause, ther is alwaies either two or 3 shallops about the killing of one whale, that the one of them maie relieve and take in the men out of another, being splitt. When he hath receaved his deadlie wound, then he casteth forth blood where formelie he spowted water; and, before he dies, he will sometimes draw the shallops 3 or 4 miles from the place where he was first stricken with the harping-iron. When he is dyeing, he most comonlie tourneth his bellie uppermost;

and then doe the men fasten a rope, or small hauser, to the hinder parte of his bodie, and with their shallops (made fast, one to another) they towe him to the ships, with his taile foremost; and then they fasten him to the sterne of some ship apointed for that purpose, where he is cutte up in manner as followeth: Two or three men came in a boate, or shallop, to the side of the whale; one man holdeing the boat close to the whale with a boat-hook, and another — who stands either in the boat or upon the whale—cutts and scores the fatt, which we call blubber, in square-like pieces, 3 or 4 feet long, with a great cutting-knife. Then, to raise it from the flesh, ther is a crab, or capstowe sett purposely upon the poop of the ship, from whence ther descends a rope, with an iron hook in the end of it; and this hook is made to take fast hould of a piece of the fatt or blubber: and as, by touring the capstowe, it is raised and lifted up, the cutter with his long knife, looseth it from the flesh, even as if the larde of a swine were, it is in this manner cleane cutt off, then doe they lower the capstowe, and lett it downe to float upon the water, makeing a hole in some side or corner of it, whereby they fasten it upon a rope. And so they proceed to cutt off more peeces; makeing fast together 10 or twelve of them at once, to be towed ashoare, at the sterne of a boat or shallop. Theise pieces, being brought to the shoare-side, are, one by one, drawen upon the shoare by the helpe of a high crane ther place; and at length are hoised up from the ground over a vessell, which is sett to receave to oil that runnes from it as it is cutt into smaller pieces; for, whilest it hangeth thus in the crane, two men doe cutt it into little peices about a foot long and half a foot thick, and putt them in the aforesaid vessel; from which it is carried to the *choppers* by two boies, who, with little flesh hooks, take in ech hand a peice, and so conveie it into tubbs, or old casks, which stand behind the *choppers*; out of which tubbs it is taken againe, and is laid for them, as they are readie to use it, upon the same board they stand on.

The *choppers* stand at the side of a shallop, which is raised from the ground and sett up of an equall height with the coppers, and stands about two yards distant from the fournaces. Then a fir-deale is laid alongst the one side of the shallop, within-board; and upon it doe they set their chopping-blocks, which are made of the whale's taile, or els of his swimming-finne. Nowe the blubber is laid readie for them by some apointed for that purpose, as before is sett downe, in such small pieces as the boies doe bring from the crane. And so they take it up with little hand-hooks, laieing it upon their blocks; where, with chopping knives, they chop it into verye small pieces, about a ynch and a halfe square. Then with a short thing of wood, made in fashion like a cole-rake, they put the chopt blubber off from the blocke downe into the shallop; out of the which it is taken againe with a copper ladle and filled into a great tubb, which hangs upon the arme of a gibbett that is made to tourne to and againe between the blubber-boat and the coppers. This tubb containeth as much blubbers as will serve one of the coppers at one boiling; and therefore, so soon as it is emptied, it is presentlie filled againe, that it maie be readie to be putt into the copper when the frittires are taken out. Theise frittires (as wee call them) are the small peices of chopt blubber, which, when the oile is sufficientlie boiled, will look browne, as if they were fried; and they are taken out of the coppers, together with some of the oile, by copper ladles, and put into a wicker basket that stands over another shallop which is placed on the other side of the fournaces, and serves as a cooler to receave the oile being drayned thorow the said basketts. And this shallop, because it receaves the oil hott out of the two coppers, is kept continuallie half full of water; which is not onelie a meanes to coole the oile before it runnes into cask, but also to clense it from soot and dross which discends to the bottome of the boat. And out of this shallop the oile runneth into a long trough, or gutter, of wood, and thereby is conveyed into butts and hogsheads; which, being filled, are bung'd up, marked, and rowl'd by, and others sett in their place. Then is the bung taken out againe, that the oile maie coole; for notwithstanding ye shallop is half full of water, yet, the coppers being continuallie plied, the oile keeps very hott in the boat, and runs also hott into the cask, which sometimes is an occasion of great leakage. Now concerning the finnes.

When the whale lies floateing at the sterne of the ship, where he is cutt up, they cut of his head, containing his toung and his finnes, comonlie called *whalebone*; and by a boat, or shallop, they twoe it so neare the shoare as it can come, and ther lett it lie till the water flowe again; for, at high waters, it is drawn further and further upon the shoare by crabs and capstowes ther placed for that purpose, untill, at a lowe water, men maie come to cutt out the finnes; which thing they doe with hatchetts, by 5 or 6 finnes at once. And theise are trailed further up from the shoare-side, and then severed ech one from another with hatchetts, and by one, at once, are laid upon a fir-deale, or other board, raised up a convenient height for a man to stand at, who scrapeth off the white pithie substance that is upon the roots, or great ends, of the finnes, with such scraping-irons as coopers use, being instruments very fitting for that purpose. Then are they rubbed in the sand, to clense them from grease which they receave when the heads are brought to the shoare-side: for, whilest the whale is in cutting up, his head is under the water, and his finnes remaine cleane; but being brought neare the shoare and grounded, then doth the grease cleave unto them at the ebbing or falling of the water, which is alwaies fattie with blubber that floats upon it continuallie. When the finnes are thus made cleane they are sorted into 5 severall kindes, and are made up into bundells of 50, contayneing of ech sorte 10 finnes. These bundles are bound up with coards; and upon ech of them ther is tied a stick, whereon is written some number, and the companie's mark sett; and so they are made readie to be shipped.

W. Martin Conway, *No Man's Land: a History of Spitsbergen from its Discovery in 1596 to the Beginning of the Scientific Explorations of the*

Country (Cambridge: Cambridge University Press, 1906), pp. 85-89.

In his tales of voyages published in London in 1744, Awnsham Churchill gives a description similar to Fotherby's (Clifford W. Ashley, *The Yankee Whaler* [Boston: Houghton Mifflin, 1926], p. 95). However the method of cutting up the whale is different, and the animal is hoisted onto shore using winches (Fig. 9) – a method more like the one employed by the Dutch.

NOTES

Introduction

1   Leonard Engel, The Sea (New York: Time Inc., 1961), p. 169.
2   The percentage of diet taken from the sea was higher in the Middle Ages. Since then, progress in agriculture and animal husbandry, together with less rigid observance of religious proscriptions, have reduced the role of fish in our diet. However, fish still dominate the diet of coastal peoples.

Precursors

1   La Grande Encyclopédie: inventaire raisonné des sciences, des lettres et des arts, s.v. "Baleine."
2   Grahame Clark, "Whales as an Economic Factor in Prehistoric Europe," Antiquity, Vol. 21, No. 82 (June 1947), p. 84.
3   E.J. Slijper, Whales (London: Hutchinson, 1962), p. 11.
4   Jacques-Yves Cousteau et Philippe Diolé, Nos amies les baleines ([Paris]: Flammarion, 1972), p. 270.
5   R.B. Robertson, Of Whales and Men (New York: Alfred A. Knopf, 1954), p. 101; J.J. Cook and W.L. Wisner, Warrior Whale (New York: Dodd, Mead, 1966), p. 55; Ivan T. Sanderson, Follow the Whale (Boston: Little Brown, 1956), p. 39. These writers, and others, state that the Phoenicians hunted sperm whales. It is also possible that the Biscayne whale was hunted at this time, and even earlier, because it was so docile.
6   Diderot, Encyclopédie ou dictionnaire raisonné des sciences, des arts et des métiers (Paris: Briasson, 1751), p. 35.
7   Ivan T. Sanderson, op. cit., p. 39. It is probably from this period and this region that the story of Jonah comes. Nowhere in the text — apparently inspired by Assyrian sources — is a whale mentioned; the word in question apparently means "big fish." In the story the fear and powerlessness in the face of the Leviathan may simply have a symbolic meaning. In the apocalyptic vision of the Ascension of Isaiah, the Leviathan represents pagan forces that must submit to Yahweh.
8   Ibid.
9   S.B.J. Noël, Histoire générale des pêches anciennes et modernes (Paris: Imprimerie Royale, 1815), p. 24.
10 Ivan T. Sanderson, op. cit., p. 33.
11 S.B.J. Noël, op. cit., p. 139.
12 Lucien Musset, "Quelques notes sur les baleiniers normands du Xe au XIIIe siècle," Revue d'histoire économique et sociale, Vol. 42, No. 2 (1964), p. 148.
13 Ibid.
14 Ibid.
15 Ibid., p. 151.

16 Ibid., p. 154.
17 S.B.J. Noël, op. cit., p. 235.
18 Lucien Musset, op. cit., p. 149.
19 Ivan T. Sanderson, op. cit., p. 84.
20 Ibid., p. 79.
21 P. Budker, Whales and Whaling (London: G.G. Harrap, 1958), p. 100.
22 J. Ross Browne, Etchings of a Whaling Cruise with Notes of a Sojourn in the Island of Zanzibar to which is Appended a Brief History of the Whale Fishery, its Past and Present Condition (New York: Harper & Brothers, 1846), p. 512.
23 Charles M. Scammon, The Marine Mammals of the Northwestern Coast of North America Described and Illustrated, Together with an Account of the American Whale-fishery (New York: Dover, 1968), p. 186n.
24 Grahame Clark, op. cit., p. 86.
25 E.J. Slijper, op. cit., p. 16.
26 Charles M. Scammon, loc. cit.
27 S.B.J. Noël, op. cit., p. 221.
28 Ivan T. Sanderson, op. cit., p. 89.
29 S.B.J. Noël, op. cit., p. 223.

The Basques

1   A further study, to be published later, will deal solely with Basque whaling. No distinction is made in the present study between the French and Spanish Basques, though most of the documentation is French.
2   Ivan T. Sanderson, op. cit., p. 133.
3   Maxime Dégros, "La grande pêche basque des origines à la fin du XVIIIe siècle," Bulletin de la Société des sciences, des arts et lettres de Bayonne, No. 35 (1940), p. 162.
4   Ibid.
5   Leonard Harrison Matthews, The Whale (London: Allen & Unwin, 1968), p. 96.
6   Clement Markham, "On the Whale-Fisheries of the Basque Provinces of Spain," Nature, Vol. 25 (1882), p. 366.
7   Maxime Dégros, op. cit., No. 35 (1940), p. 163.
8   William Scoresby, The Arctic Regions and the Northern Whalefishery (London: The Religious Tract Society, [1824]) (hereafter cited as Arctic Regions), p. 11.
9   S.B.J. Noël, op. cit., p. 230.
10 Lucien Musset, op. cit., p. 161.
11 Grand dictionnaire universel, s.v. "Baleine."
12 William Scoresby, Arctic Regions, p. 14.
13 Jean Laborde, "La pêche à la baleine par les harponneurs basques," Gure Herria Hogoi-ta-Hiaugarren Urthea, No. 5 (1951), p. 261.
14 Clement Markham, op. cit., p. 366.
15 Jean Laborde, loc. cit.
16 William Scoresby, Arctic Regions, p. 14.
17 S.B.J. Noël, op. cit., p. 15.
18 Édouard Ducéré, Dictionnaire historique de Bayonne, 2nd ed. (Marseille: 1974), s.v. "Baleine."

19 It is difficult to distinguish French and Spanish Basques during the High Middle Ages. The two peoples signed several trade agreements, even in war. They also helped each other, even going so far as to exchange nationalities when one of the two nations was at war with a third (Maxime Dégros, op. cit., [1940], p. 165).

20 Ivan T. Sanderson, op. cit., p.130.

21 Maxime Dégros, op. cit., No. 35 (1940), p. 167.

22 Fernand Braudel, Civilisation matérielle et capitalisme; XVe-XVIIIe siècles ([Paris]: Armand Colin, 1967), p. 162.

23 Ibid., p. 156.

24 E. Cleirac, Us et coutumes de la mer (Rouen: Jean Lucas, 1671), p. 129.

25 It is tempting to see a link between the beginnings of these long voyages and the appearance of navigating instruments in the late 15th and early 16th centuries. But according to Jacques Heers (Christophe Colomb [Paris: Hachette, 1981]), this theory springs more from a desire to glorify technology and reduce the role of heroic individuals than from analysis of the facts. The compass undoubtedly played a role (all pilots had the use of one by this time), but it had been used regularly and relatively correctly in the West since at least the 13th century. The astrolabe, on the other hand, was still not well known and it seems that it could give exact measurements only on land, not on board ship. Regarding the determination of longitude, mariners' experience was just as helpful as the sandclocks that were employed. Navigation, in short, was not yet a science; it was still an art whose success depended on the empirical knowledge helmsmen acquired in the course of numerous voyages. No mariner could really say exactly what his latitude and longitude were when at sea.

26 J.-B. Bailac, Nouvelle chronique de la ville de Bayonne (Bayonne: Duhard-Fauvet, 1827), p. 57.

27 Mario Ruspoli, À la recherche du cachalot (Paris: Éditions de Paris, 1955), p. 66.

28 Maxime Dégros, op. cit., No. 35 (1940), p. 172.

29 Ibid., p. 168. Mentioned in a document of 1775 in the archives of the French department of Basses Pyrénées (C. 336). A document of 1715 in the municipal archives of Saint-Jean-de-Luz mentions the year 1392.

30 In the early 16th century, "Terre-Neuve" (New Found Land) had a very broad sense. For instance, a document of that time says "Il est tout certain et notoire que mariniers vont ... es terres neufves.... En terre neufve a de bons ports et hables, Meilleurs deurope et fort belles rivieres, Grant pescherie...." (It is quite certain and well known that mariners go ... to the new lands.... In the new land are good ports and harbours, better than in Europe, and very beautiful rivers, huge fishing grounds....") (René Bélanger, Les Basques dans l'estuaire du Saint-Laurent [Montreal: Les Presses de l'université du Québec, 1971], p. 35).

31 Maxime Dégros, op. cit., No. 35 (1940), p. 167.

32 Ibid.

33 René Bélanger, op. cit., p. 90.

34 The Basques are not alone in claiming to have discovered America before Columbus. The Bretons and Normans make similar claims. During a trial involving the Abbot of Fécamp and a shipowner from Selles, the latter states that in 1487 Harfleur was a port "where all the ships that fish for cod in the new lands arrive" (Éric Dardel, État des pêches maritimes sur les côtes occidentales de la France au début du XVIIIe siècle [Paris: André Tournon, 1941], p. 107.

35 René Bélanger, op. cit., p. 36.

36 Ibid.

37 F. Michel, Le Pays basque (Paris: Firmin Diderot, 1857), p. 188.

38 Paul Gaffarel, Voyages des Français au Canada dans l'Amérique centrale et au Brésil dans les premières années du XVIe siècle (Lausanne: Imprimeries Réunies, 1972), p. 215n.

39 David S. Henderson, Fishing for the Whale; A Guide-catalogue to the Collection of Whaling Relics in Dundee Museum (Dundee: Dundee Museum and Art Gallery, 1972), p. 8.

40 James Travis Jenkins, A History of the Whale Fisheries (London: H.F. and G. Witherby, 1921), p. 74.

41 René Bélanger, op. cit., p. 46

42 According to René Bélanger (loc. cit.), Hoyarsabal named the port in Red Bay "Ballenne." Actually the place so called was apparently present-day Carrolls Cove.

43 James Travis Jenkins, op. cit., p. 68.

44 In 1631 Guipuzcoa was no longer sending even a single ship to Newfoundland.

45 Marcel Moussette, "La pêche à la baleine; méthodes de capture de la baleine utilisées dans le golfe et l'estuaire du Saint-Laurent," Revue d'histoire de la Gaspésie, Vol. 10, No. 1 (Jan.-Mar. 1972), p. 19.

46 N. Fauteux, "Privilège exclusif pour la pêche à la baleine," Bulletin des recherches historiques, Vol. 52, No. 3 (Mar. 1946), p. 79.

47 Claude-Charles Le Roy de Bacqueville de la Potherie, Histoire de l'Amérique septentrionale (Paris: Jean-Luc Nion, 1722), p. 276; Marcel Moussette, op. cit., p. 19.

48 René Bélanger, op. cit., p. 49.

49 Ibid., p. 66.

50 Ibid., p. 78.

51 Ibid., p. 77.

52 W. Martin Conway, No Man's Land: A History of Spitsbergen from its Discovery in 1596 to the Beginning of the Scientific Explorations of the Country (Cambridge: Cambridge University Press, 1906), p. 42.

53 S. Purchas, Hakluytus Posthumus, or, Purchas His Pilgrimes (Glasgow: Hakluyt Society, 1906), p. 31.

54 Clement Markham, op. cit., p. 367.

55 W. Martin Conway, op. cit., p. 52.

56 F. Michel, op. cit., p. 191n.

57 Ibid.

58 Clement Markham, Voyages of William Baffin, 1612-1622 (London: Hakluyt Society, 1881), p. 40.

59 René Bélanger, op. cit., p. 78.

60 F. Michel, op. cit., p. 190.
61 Ibid., p. 192.
62 Ibid., p. 190.
63 Éric Dardel, op. cit., p. 130.
64 Maxime Dégros, op. cit., No. 35 (1940), p. 157.
65 Ibid., No. 44 (1943), p. 96.
66 Éric Dardel, op. cit., p. 132.

The English
1   Ivan T. Sanderson, op. cit., p. 151.
2   J. Ross Browne, op. cit., p. 512.
3   B. Henry Révoil, Pêches dans l'Amérique du Nord (Paris: Hachette, 1863), p. 192.
4   Spitsbergen was called "Greenland" by Barents, and then by Hudson, because they thought it was an extension of what we now know as Greenland. Among whalers, the name "Greenland" continued to be used in this way until the 19th century.
5   English historians generally deny that Spitsbergen was discovered by Barents, claiming instead that Hudson discovered it in 1607. The error stems from John Playse, who transcribed extracts from Hudson's diary into his own. Hudson himself never claimed to have discovered Spitsbergen.
6   Russia towards Muscovy and St. Nicholas. The killing of the whale is both pleasant and profitable, and without great charges, yielding great plenty of oil, the tun where of is worth ten pounds" (Gordon Jackson, The British Whaling Trade [Hamden: Archon Books, 1978], p. 5).
7   W. Martin Conway, op. cit., p. 35.
8   Gordon Jackson, op. cit., p. 7.
9   S. Purchas, op. cit., p. 12.
10 Henry Elking, View of the Greenland Trade and Whale-fishery (London: J. Roberts, 1722), p. 41.
11 David S. Henderson, op. cit., p. 110.
12 John Narborough, An Account of Several Late Voyages and Discoveries to the South and North.... (London: Sam Smith, 1694), p. 166.
13 Charles Boardman Hawes, Whaling (London: W. Heinemann, 1924), pp. 339-41.
14 E.J. Slijper, op. cit., p. 19.
15 Gordon Jackson, op. cit., p. 20.
16 Ibid., p. 21.
17 James Travis Jenkins, op. cit., p. 163.
18 Ivan T. Sanderson, op. cit., p. 154.
19 W. Martin Conway, op. cit., p. 178.
20 Four tons of blubber yields three tons of oil.
21 W. Martin Conway, op. cit., p. 203.
22 William Scoresby, Arctic Regions, p. 103.
23 Ibid., p. 25.
24 Henry Elking, op. cit., p. 49.
25 According to Scoresby, because of the ambiguity of the word "Greenland," it is impossible to determine whether the English

were hunting east of Greenland or in Davis Strait, and it is even impossible to say in what year they began to hunt in Davis Strait (Arctic Regions, p. 115). The distinction is really of no great importance.

26 James Travis Jenkins, op. cit., p. 183.
27 William Scoresby, Arctic Regions, p. 105.
28 Ibid., p. 20.
29 Gordon Jackson, op. cit., p. 52.
30 William Scoresby, Arctic Regions, p. 26.
31 Gordon Jackson, op. cit., p. 91.
32 William Scoresby, An Account of the Arctic Regions with a History and Description of the Northern Whale-fishery (Edinburgh: Archibald Constable, 1820) (hereafter cited as Account), Vol. 2, p. 137.
33 Between 1733 and 1785, England spent £1,265,461 on bounties (ibid., p. 110).
34 William Scoresby, Arctic Regions, p. 117.
35 Gordon Jackson, op. cit., p. 70.
36 Ibid., p. 82.
37 David S. Henderson, op. cit., p. 11.
38 Ibid.
39 Jackson R.E. Scoresby, The Life of William Scoresby (London: T. Nelson and Sons, 1861).
40 William Scoresby, Account, Vol. 2, p. 507.
41 John Leslie, Narrative of Discovery and Adventure in the Polar Seas and Regions.... (Edinburgh: Oliver & Boyd, 1835), p. 443.
42 E. Keble Chatterton, Whalers and Whaling: The Story of the Whaling Ships up to the Present Day (Philadelphia: J.B. Lippincott, 1926), p. 24.
43 William Scoresby, Arctic Regions, p. 123.
44 One gallon of whale oil equalled 2.40 cubic metres of gas.
45 La Grande Encyclopédie, s.v. "Baleine."

The Dutch

1 S. Purchas, op. cit., p. 12.
2 Henry Elking, op. cit., p. 41.
3 S. Purchas, op. cit., p. 17.
4 William Scoresby, Account, Vol. 2, p. 33.
5 Ibid., p. 143. According to Sir W. Martin Conway, the number of hunters at Smeerenberg has been greatly exaggerated. He says there were never more than 1000 to 1200 (W. Martin Conway, op. cit., p. 138).
6 W. Martin Conway, op. cit., p. 137.
7 James Travis Jenkins, op. cit., p. 127.
8 Ivan T. Sanderson, op. cit., 168. The use of seasonal bases was probably inspired by earlier European experiments. Such bases reportedly existed in Flanders as early as 875 (ibid., p. 165).
9 Charles Boardman Hawes, op. cit., p. 23.
10 W. Martin Conway, op. cit., p. 191.
11 James Travis Jenkins, op. cit., p. 136.
12 Henry Elking, op. cit., p. 38.

13 F.V. Morley and J.S. Hodgson, Whaling North and South (London: Methuen, 1927), p. 52.

14 William Scoresby, Account, Vol. 2, p. 105.

15 Basil Lubbock, The Arctic Whalers (Glasgow: Brown, Son & Ferguson, 1937), p. 81.

16 Henry Elking, op. cit., p. 39.

17 According to Diderot, three casks of blubber gave one cask of oil. Thus a Basque ship would bring back three times as much as a Dutch ship of the same capacity (Diderot, op. cit., p. 311). The 3:1 ratio appears to be exaggerated (cf note 20 of the preceding chapter).

18 John Leslie, op. cit., p. 424.

19 Ivan T. Sanderson, op. cit., p. 172.

20 According to Scoresby (Account, Vol. 2, p. 94n), a quardeel equalled 12 Dutch stecken or 60.27 English gallons.

21 Diderot, op. cit., p. 35.

22 Duhamel du Monceau, Traité général des pêches et histoire des poissons qu'elles fournissent tant pour la subsistance des hommes que pour plusieurs autres usages qui ont rapport aux arts et au commerce (Paris: Desaint, 1782), Vol. 4, p. 27.

23 James Travis Jenkins, op. cit., p. 167.

24 Éric Dardel, op. cit., p. 130.

25 James Travis Jenkins, op. cit., p. 168.

26 Diderot, op. cit., p. 35.

27 James Travis Jenkins, op. cit., p. 197.

28 William Scoresby, Account, Vol. 2, p. 156.

The Americans

1   Alexander Starbuck, History of the American Whale-fishery from its Earliest Inception to the Year 1876 (New York: Argosy-Antiquarian, 1964), Vol. 1, p. 5n.

2   Ibid.

3   Glover M. Allen, "The Whalebone Whales of New England," Memoirs of the Boston Society of Natural History, Vol. 8, No. 2 (1916), p. 147.

4   Charles M. Scammon, op. cit., p. 202.

5   Dauril Alden, "Yankee Sperm Whalers in Brazilian Waters, and the Decline of the Portuguese Whale Fishery, 1773-1801," The Americas: A Quarterly Review of Inter-american Cultural History, Vol. 20, No. 3 (Jan. 1964), p. 273.

6   George Waymouth, "A True Relation of the Most Prosperous Voyage Made this Present Year, 1605, by Captain George Waymouth in the Discovery of the Land of Virginia...," Collections of the Massachusetts Historical Society, 3rd ser., Vol. 8 (1843), p. 156.

7   E.P. Hohman, The American Whaleman (Clifton: Augustus M. Kelley, 1972), p. 25.

8   Ibid.

9   Ibid., p. 24.

10 Alexander Starbuck, op. cit., p. 15.

11 Dauril Alden, op. cit., p. 273.

12 E.P. Hohman, op. cit., p. 26.
13 Irwin Shapiro, Story of Yankee Whaling (New York: American Heritage, 1959), p. 15.
14 E.P. Hohman, op. cit., p. 26.
15 Foster Rhea Dulles, Lowered Boats; A Chronicle of American Whaling (New York: Harcourt, Brace, 1933), p. 31.
16 Edouard A. Stackpole, The Sea-Hunters: The New England Whalemen during Two Centuries, 1635-1835 (New York: J.B. Lippincott, 1953), p. 21.
17 Clifford W. Ashley, The Yankee Whaler (Boston: Houghton Mifflin, 1926), p. 96.
18 . Hohman, op. cit., p. 26.
19 J. Ross Browne, op. cit., p. 517.
20 Glover M. Allen, op. cit., p. 160.
21 Dauril Alden, op. cit., p. 273.
22 Alexander Starbuck, op. cit., Vol. 2, p. 661n.
23 Foster Rhea Dulles, op. cit., p. 33.
24 A. Hyatt Verrill, The Real Story of the Whaler (New York: D. Appleton, 1916), p. 33.
25 Alexander Starbuck, op. cit., Vol. 1, p. 20.
26 Ivan T. Sanderson, op. cit., p. 212.
27 Alexander Starbuck, op. cit., Vol. 1, p. 22.
28 The English subsidies applied to all foreign Protestant ships less than two years old hunting in Greenland and delivering their cargoes to Great Britain.
29 Dauril Alden, op. cit., p. 275.
30 Edouard Stackpole, op. cit., p. 31.
31 E.P. Hohman, op. cit., p. 28.
32 Clifford W. Ashley, op. cit., p. 47.
33 James Temple Brown, "Whalemen, Vessels, Apparatus and Methods of the Fishery" in George Brown Goode, The Fisheries and Fishery Industries of the United States (Washington: Government Printing Office, 1884-87).
34 Clifford W. Ashley, op. cit., p. 96.
35 No less than 90 whalers apparently participated in the attack on Quebec City in 1759; Gordon Jackson, op. cit., p. 65.
36 William Scoresby, Account, Vol. 2, p. 135.
37 Alexander Starbuck, op. cit., Vol. 1, p. 44.
38 Ibid., p. 45.
39 Ibid., p. 47.
40 Edouard Stackpole, op. cit., p. 48.
41 E.P. Hohman, op. cit., p. 32.
42 Ibid., p. 33.
43 The first authorization to hunt was not granted until 1781.
44 E.P. Hohman, op. cit., p. 38.
45 Ibid., p. 39.
46 F.V. Morley and J.S. Hodgson, op. cit., p. 60.
47 Ibid.
48 Charles M. Scammon, op. cit., p. 212.
49 E.P. Hohman, op. cit., p. 41.
50 J. Ross Browne, op. cit., p. 539.

51 F.V. Morley and J.S. Hodgson, loc. cit.
52 Charles M. Scammon, op. cit., p. 212.
53 Foster Rhea Dulles, op. cit., p. 198.
54 E.P. Hohman, op. cit., p. 41.
55 Charles M. Scammon, op. cit., p. 312.
56 The Truelove, built in Philadelphia in 1764, made 72 journeys.
57 Foster Rhea Dulles, op. cit., p. 80.
58 E.P. Hohman, op. cit., p. 240.
59 Foster Rhea Dulles, op. cit., p. 93.
60 Robert Owen Decker, Whaling Industry of New London (York: Liberty Cap Books, 1973), p. 91.
61 E.P. Hohman, op. cit., p. 85.
62 Foster Rhea Dulles, op. cit., p. 156.
63 Ibid., p. 117.
64 Charles M. Scammon, op. cit., p. 224.
65 Ibid.
66 Ibid., p. 227.
67 Clifford W. Ashley, op. cit., p. 93.
68 James Temple Brown, op. cit., p. 262.
69 Herman Melville, Moby Dick, or, The Whale (Franklin Centre: The Franklin Library, 1974), p. 387.
70 A.H. Clark, "History and Present Condition of the Fishery," in G.B. Goode, op. cit., p. 7.
71 A. Hyatt Verrill, op. cit., p. 219.
72 F.V. Morley and J.S. Hodgson, op. cit., p. 65.
73 J. Ross Browne, op. cit., p. iv.

Conclusion
1 F.V. Morley and J.S. Hodgson, op. cit., p. 74.
2 Paul Budker, Whales and Whaling (London: G.G. Harrap, 1958), p. 157.
3 La Cepède, Histoire naturelle des cétacés (Paris: Plassan, Year XII of the Republic), p. xxxi.

BIBLIOGRAPHY

Alden, Dauril
"Yankee Sperm Whalers in Brazilian Waters, and the Decline of the Portuguese Whale Fishery, 1773-1801." The Americas: A Quarterly Review of Inter-American Cultural History, Vol. 20, No. 3 (Jan. 1964), pp. 267-88.

Allen, Glover M.
"The Whalebone Whales of New England." Memoirs of the Boston Society of Natural History, Vol. 8, No. 2 (1916), pp. 105-322.

Allen, J.A.
"The North Atlantic Right Whale and its Near Allies." Bulletin of the American Museum of Natural History, Vol. 24 (1908), pp. 277-329.

Anderson, George
"A Whale is Killed." The Beaver, Vol. 277, No. 4 (Mar. 1947), pp. 18-21.

Anderson, J.W.
"The Whales of the St. Lawrence." The Canadian Naturalist, Vol. 6, No. 2 (1872), pp. 203-208.

Andrews, Clarence L.
"Alaska Whaling." Washington Historical Quarterly, Vol. 9, No. 1 (Jan. 1918), pp. 3-10.

Andrews, Roy Chapman
Whale Hunting with Gun and Camera. D. Appleton, New York, 1931.

Arne, P.
"La baleine des Basques." Bulletin du Musée basque, Vols. 18-19, Nos. 21-22 (1942-43), pp. 189-96.

Ash, Christopher
Whaler's Eye. Macmillan, New York, 1962.

Ashley, Clifford W.
The Yankee Whaler. Houghton Mifflin, Boston, 1926.

Bailac, Jean-Baptiste
Nouvelle chronique de la ville de Bayonne. Duhart-Fauvet, Bayonne, 1827.

Barkham, Selma
"Building Materials for Canada." Bulletin of the Association for Preser-

vation Technology, Vol. 5, No. 4 (1973), pp. 93-94.
---. "The Spanish Province of Terranova," Manuscript on file, National Historic Parks and Sites Branch, Parks Canada, Ottawa, 1974.

Barron, William
An Apprentice's Reminiscences of Whaling in Davis Straits: Narrative of the Voyages of the Hull Barque Truelove, 1848-1854. M. Waller, Hull, England, 1890.
---. Old Whaling Days. Conway Maritime Press, Cardiff, 1970.

Baudrillart, J.J.
Traité général des eaux et forêts, chasses et pêches. Arthur Bertrand, Paris, 1827.

Beale, Thomas
The Natural History of the Sperm Whale. Holland Press, London, 1973.

Beddard, F.E.
A Book of Whales. J. Murray, London, 1900.

Bélanger, René
Les Basques dans l'estuaire du Saint-Laurent. Les Presses de l'université du Québec, Montreal, 1971.

Bell, J.J.
The Whalers. Hodder & Stoughton, London, 1914.

Bellet, Adolphe
La grande pêche de la morue à Terre-Neuve depuis la découverte du Nouveau Monde par les Basques au XIVᵉ siècle. Augustin Challamel, Paris, 1902.

Bennett, F. Debell
Narrative of a Whaling Voyage Round the Globe, 1833-1836. Bentley, London, 1840.

Bernard, Jacques
Navires et gens de mer à Bordeaux, 1400-1550. SEUPEN, Paris, 1968.

Blond, Georges
La grande aventure des baleines. Amiot-Dumont, Ottawa, 1953.

Bockstone, John R.
Steam Whaling in the Western Arctic. Dartmouth Historical Society, New Bedford, 1977.

Bodfish, Hartson Hartlell
Chasing Bowhead. Harvard University Press, Cambridge, 1936.

Boissonnade, P.
"La marine de commerce et de pêche du Pays basque et du Labourd au

temps de Colbert." Bulletin de la section de géographie du Comité des travaux historiques et scientifiques, Vol. 49 (1934), pp. 43-87.

Bosworth, Allan R.
Storm Tide. Harper & Row, New York, 1965.

Boucault, Sieur
"État présent du Canada (1754)." Rapport des Archives du Québec (1920-1921), pp. 11-50.

Brandt, Karl
"Whale Oil, An Economic Analysis." Fats and Oils Studies, No. 7 (1940).
---. Whaling and Whale Oil during and after World War II. Food Research Institute, Stanford,1948.

Braudel, Fernand
Civilisation matérielle et capitalisme; XVe- XVIIIe siècles. Armand Colin, [Paris], 1967.

Brown, James Temple
The Whale Fishery and its Appliances. Government Printing Office, Washington, 1883.

Brown, Richard
Notes on the Northern Atlantic, for the Use of Travellers. Sampson, London, 1880

Brown, Robert N.R.
"The Commercial Development of Spitsbergen." Scottish Geographical Journal Magazine, Vol. 28 (Nov. 1912), pp. 561-71.
---. The Polar Regions, A Physical and Economic Geography of the Arctic and Antarctic. Methuen, London, 1927.

Browne, J. Ross
Etchings of a Whaling Cruise with Notes of a Sojourn on the Island of Zanzibar to which is Appended a Brief History of the Whale Fishery, its Past and Present Condition. Harper & Brothers, New York, 1846.

Browne, P.W.
Where the Fishers Go; The Story of Labrador. Cochrane, New York, 1909.

Budker, Paul
"Baleines et baleinoptères." Naturalia, No. 6 (Mar. 1954), pp. 28-31.
---. Whales and Whaling. G.G. Harrap, London, 1958.

Bullen, F.T.
The Cruise of the "Cachalot"; Round the World after Sperm Whales. Smith, Elder, London, 1901.

Burton, Robert
The Life and Death of Whales. A. Deutsch, London, 1973.

Butel-Dumont, G.M.
Histoire et commerce des colonies anglaises dans l'Amérique septentrionale. Le Breton, London, 1755.

Canada. Department of Fisheries and Oceans.
The Biology and Hunting of Beluga or White Whales in the Canadian
Arctic. Montreal, 1962.

Canada (Province). Legislative Assembly.
"Rapport annuel de Pierre Fortin, magistrat commandant l'expédition
pour la protection des pêcheries dans le golfe Saint-Laurent pendant la
saison 1861-1862." In Documents de la session, No. 11 (1862), Hunter
Rose, Quebec City, 1862.

Chatterton, E. Keble
Whalers and Whaling: The Story of the Whaling Ships up to the Present
Day. J.B. Lippincott, Philadelphia, 1926.

Cheever, Henry T.
The Whale and his Captors. T. Nelson & Sons, London, 1858.

Chippendale, H.A.
Sails and Whales. Houghton Mifflin, Cambridge, 1951.

Christison, Robert
"On the Capture of Whales by Means of Poison." New Philosophical
Journal, new ser., Vol. 12 (1860), pp. 72-80.

Church, Albert Cook
Whales, Ships and Whaling. Norton, New York, 1960.

Churchill, Awnsham
A Collection of Voyages and Travels. Henry Lintot, London, 1744.

Clapperton, George A.
"Il est né l'année de la baleine." Revue d'histoire de la Gaspésie, Vol. 9,
No. 3 (July-Sept. 1971), pp. 335-36.

Clark, Grahame
"Whales as an Economic Factor in Prehistoric Europe." Antiquity, Vol.
21, No. 82 (June 1947), pp. 84-104.

Clark, J.G.D.
"Seal-Hunting in the Stone Age of North Western Europe." Proceedings
of the Prehistorical Society, Vol. 12 (1946), pp. 12-48.

Clark, Robert
"Electric Whaling." Nature, Vol. 169, No. 4308 (24 May 1952), pp. 859-860.

Cleirac, Étienne
Us et coutumes de la mer. Jean Lucas, Rouen, 1671.

Cocks, Alfred Heneage
"The Finwhale Fishery of 1885 on the North European Coast." Zoologist, 3rd ser., Vols. 10-14 (1886-90).

Colnett, James
A Voyage to the South Atlantic and around Cape Horn into the Pacific Ocean for the Purpose of Extending the Spermacetti Whale Fisheries and Other Objects of Commerce. W. Bennett, London, 1798.

Colwell, M.
Whaling around Australia. 2nd ed. London, 1970.

Commission for Whaling Statistics
International Whaling Statistics. Oslo, 1930-39. Vols. 1-13.

Conway, W. Martin
Early Dutch and English Voyages to Spitsbergen in the 17th Century. The Hakluyt Society, London, 1902. Hakluyt Series, 2nd ser., No. 11.
---. No Man's Land: A History of Spitsbergen from its Discovery in 1596 to the Beginning of the Scientific Explorations of the Country. Cambridge University Press, Cambridge, 1906.

Cook, John Atkins
Pursuing the Whale; A Quarter-century of Whaling in the Arctic. Houghton Mifflin, Boston, 1926.

Cook, John Atkins, and S.S. Pederson
Thar she Blows. Chapman & Gumes, Boston, 1937.

Cook, J.J., and W.L. Wisner
Warrior Whale. Dodd, Mead, New York, 1966.

Cousteau, Jacques-Yves, and Philippe Diolé
Nos amies les baleines. Flammarion, [Paris], 1972.

Crisp, Frank
The Adventure of Whaling. Macmillan, London, 1954.

D'Abartiagne, William
"L'Atlantique et les Basques." Bulletin de la Société des sciences, lettres et arts de Bayonne, No. 22 (1937), pp. 262-73.

Dakin, William John
Whalemen Adventurers. Angus & Robertson, Sydney, 1934.

Dardel, Éric
État des pêches maritimes sur les côtes occidentales de la France au début du XVIIIe siècle. D'après les procès-verbaux de visite de l'Inspecteur des pêches, Le Masson du Parc, 1723-1732. André Tournon, Paris, 1941.

Davis, William
Nimrod of the Sea, or, The American Whaleman. Charles E. Lauriat, Boston, 1926.

Decker, R.
The Whaling City. Pequot Press, Chester, 1976.

Decker, Robert Owen
Whaling Industry of New London. Liberty Cap Books, York, 1973.

Dégros, Maxime
"La grande pêche basque des origines à la fin du XVIIIe siècle." Bulletin de la Société des sciences, des arts et lettres de Bayonne, Nos. 35-50, 1940-45.

De Reste, Bernard
Histoire des pêches, des découvertes et des établissements des Hollandais dans les mers du Nord. Nyon, Paris, 1801.

Dewhirst, John
"The Origins of Nootkan Whaling." Manuscript on file, National Historic Parks and Sites Branch, Parks Canada, Ottawa, 1977.

Diderot
Encyclopédie ou dictionnaire raisonné des sciences, des arts et des métiers. Briasson, Paris, 1751-65. 17 vols.

Doan, K.H., and C.W. Douglas
Beluga of the Churchill Region of Hudson Bay. Department of Fisheries and Oceans, Ottawa, 1953.

Dow, George Francis
Whale Ships and Whaling. A Pictorial History of Whaling during Three Centuries, with an Account of Whale Fishery in Colonial New England. Marine Research Society, No. 10, pp. i-xii. Salem.

Ducéré, Édouard
Dictionnaire historique de Bayonne. 2nd ed. Marseille, 1974.

Duhamel du Monceau
Traité général des pesches et histoire des poissons qu'elles fournissent tant pour la subsistance des hommes que pour plusieurs autres usages qui ont rapport aux arts et au commerce. Desaint, Paris, 1782.

Dulles, Foster Rhea
Lowered Boats; A Chronicle of American Whaling. Harcourt, Brace, New York, 1933.

Echegarry, Rafael Gonzalez
Balleneros Cantabros. Institucion cultural de Cantabria, Santander, 1978.

Edwards, Everett J., and J.E. Rattray
Whale Off. Frederick A. Stokes, New York, 1932.

Elking, Henry
View of the Greenland Trade and Whale-fishery. J. Roberts, London, 1722.

Engel, Leonard
The Sea. Time Incorporated, New York, 1961.

Fauteux, J.N.
Essai sur l'industrie au Canada sous le régime français. Proulx, Quebec City, 1927.

Fauteux, N.
"Privilège exclusif pour la pêche à la baleine." Bulletin des recherches historiques, Vol. 52, No. 3 (Mar. 1946), pp. 78-79.

Ferguson, Robert
Arctic Harpooner; A Voyage on the Schooner Abbie Bradford, 1878-1879. University of Pennsylvania, Philadelphia, 1938.

Ferland, J.B.A.
Le Labrador; notes et récits de voyage. Beauchemin, Montreal, 1858.

Figuier, Louis
L'art de l'éclairage. Jouvert, Paris, 1887.

Fischer, M.
"Cétacés du Sud-Ouest de la France." Actes de la Société Linnéenne, 4th ser., Vol. 35, No. 5 (1881), pp. 5-219.

Fitter, Richard
Les animaux sauvages en voie de disparition dans le monde. 2nd ed. Paris, 1970.

Flyger, Vagn
"Succinylcholine Chloride for Killing or Capturing Whales." Norsk hvalfangst-Tidende, No. 4 (1964), pp. 88-90.

Fourquin, Guy
Histoire économique de l'Occident médiéval. Armand Colin, Paris, 1969.

Frazer, F.C.
"Early Japanese Whaling." Proceedings of the Linnean Society of London (1937), pp. 19-20.

Gaffarel, Paul
Voyages des Français au Canada dans l'Amérique centrale et au Brésil dans les premières années du XVIe siècle. Imprimeries Réunies, Lausanne, 1972.

Gallop, Rodney
A Book of the Basques. University of Nevada Press, Reno, 1930.

Gardi, René
Chasse à la baleine. V. Attinger, Paris, 1948.

Gardner, G.
"La pêche à Terre-Neuve." Actualité économique, Vol. 2, No. 4 (Feb. 1941), pp. 322-43.

Gauroy, Pierre
"Dans le sillage des chasseurs de baleines." Naturalia, No. 2 (1953), pp. 41-44.

Giambarba, Paul
Whales, Whaling and Whale Craft. Scrimshaw Pub., Centerville, 1967.

Goode, George Brown
The Fisheries and Fishery Industries of the United States. Government Printing Office, Washington, 1884-87.

La Grande Encyclopédie: inventaire raisonné des sciences, des lettres et des arts
Société anonyme de la grande encyclopédie, Paris, n.d.

Grant, C.D.
A Descriptive Report on Technique Employed by Whalers. 2nd ed. N.p., 1947.

Gray, R.W.
"The Colour of the Greenland Sea and the Migrations of the Greenland Whale and Narwhal." Geographic Journal, Vol. 78 (Sept. 1931), pp. 284-290.

Hadley, J.
"Whaling off the Alaskan Coast." Bulletin of the American Geographical Society, Vol. 47, No. 12 (1915), pp. 905-921.

Haldane, R.C.
"Whaling in Scotland and Shetlands." Annals of the Scotland Natural History, No. 54 (Apr. 1905), No. 59 (July 1906), No. 61 (Jan. 1907), No. 66 (Apr. 1908), No. 70 (Apr. 1909), No. 73 (Jan. 1910).

Haley, Nelson Cole
Whale Hunt: The Narrative of a Voyage by NCH, Harpooner in the Ship Charles W. Morgan, 1849-53. Washburn, New York, 1967.

Hamy, E.T.
"Les Français au Spitzberg." Études historiques et géographiques (1896), pp. 309-332.

Hanssen, Helmer Julius
Voyages of A Modern Viking. George Routledge & Sons, London, 1936.

Hare, Lloyd C.M.
Salted Stories; The Story of the Whaling Fleets of San Francisco. The Marine Historical Association, Mystic, 1960.

Harmer, Sidney F.
"The History of Whaling." Proceedings of the Linnean Society, 140th session (1927-28).

Harrington, Lyn
"The Whalers of Coal Harbour." Imperial Oil (Dec. 1958), pp. 1-4.

Hawes, Charles Boardmann
Whaling. W. Heinemann, London, 1924.

Heers, Jacques
Christophe Colomb. Hachette, Paris, 1981.

Hegarty, Reginald B.
Returns of Whaling Vessels Sailing from American Ports. N.p., New Bedford, 1959.
---. The Rope's End. Houghton Mifflin, Boston, 1965.

Heizer, Robert Fleming
"A Pacific Eskimo Invention in Whale Hunting in Historic Times." American Anthropologist, Vol. 45, No. 1 (Jan.-Mar. 1943), pp. 120-22.

Henderson, David S.
Fishing for the Whale; A Guide-catalogue to the Collection of Whaling Relics in Dundee Museum. Dundee Museum & Art Gallery, Dundee, 1972.

Herubel, Marcel A.
"Baleines et baleiniers." Revue maritime (May 1931), pp. 591-633.

Hessel, Gérard A., ed.
Histoire du pays nommé Spitsberghe comment il a esté descouvert, la situation & de ses animauls avec le discours des empeschemens que les navires esquippés pour la pêche des baleines tant Basques, Hollandois, que Flamens ont soufferts de la part des Anglois en l'année présente 1613. 2nd ed. Amsterdam, 1613.

Hjort, Johan, and J.T. Rudd
"Whaling and Fishing in the North Atlantic." Conseil permanent international pour l'exploration de la mer, Vol. 56 (1929), pp. 1-123.

Hohman, E.P.
The American Whaleman. Augustus M. Kelley, Clifton, 1972.

Holmes, L.
The Arctic Whaleman. Wenworth, Boston, 1857.

Hornell, James
"Sea-trade in Early Times." Antiquity (Sept. 1941), pp. 233-56.

Hough, Henry Beetle
Great Days of Whaling. Houghton Mifflin, Boston, 1958.

Housby, Trevor R.
The Hand of God. Abelard-Schuman, London, 1971.

Howland, Chester Scott
Thar she Blows. W. Funks, New York, 1951.

Huntington, Gale
Songs the Whaleman Sang. Barre Pub., Barre, 1964.

Hyde, Alexander
The Frozen Zone and its Explorers. Columbian Book, Hartford, 1874.

Hyde, Michael
Arctic Whaling Adventures. Oxford University Press, London, 1955.

Ingerbrigtsen, A.
"Whales Caught in the North Atlantic and Other Seas." International Council for the Study of the Sea, Vol. 56, No. 2 (1929), pp. 1-26.

Jackson, Gordon
The British Whaling Trade. Archon Books, Hamden, 1978.

Jameson, William
"Narrative of a Voyage to Davis' Straits in 1820." Philosophical Journal, Vol. 5 (Oct. 1821), pp. 309-18.

Jenkins, James Travis
A History of the Whale Fisheries. H.F. and G. Witherby, London, 1921.
---. "Bibliography of Whaling." Journal of the Society for the Bibliography of Material History, Vol. 2, Part 4 (1948).
---. Whales and Modern Whaling. Witherby and Co., London, 1932.

Jones, A.
"The Whaling Trade of Bristol, 1750-1758." Bristol Chamber of Commerce Journal, Vol. 27, No. 12 (Mar. 1953), pp. 9-11.

Kerr, George
"An Arctic Whaling Journal of 1791." Polar Record, Vol. 9, No. 63 (Sept. 1959), pp. 534-46.

Laborde, Jean
"La pêche à la baleine par les harponneurs basques." Gure Herria Hogoita-Hiaugarren, No. 5 (1951).

Labrie, Arthur
"Notre territoire de pêche maritime." In Esdras Minville, Pêche et chasse, École des hautes études commerciales, Montreal, 1946.

Laccoureye, J.
"La pêche à la baleine, la pêche à la morue et la petite pêche par les Biarrots." Bulletin de Biarritz association, Vol. 11 (1906), pp. 34-130 (passim). Biarritz.

La Cepède
Histoire naturelle des cétacés. Plassan, Paris, Year XII of the Republic.

Laing, John
An Account of a Voyage to Spitsbergen. J. Mawman, London, 1815.

Lantis, Margaret
"The Alaskan Whale Cult and its Affinities." American Anthropologist, Vol. 40, No. 3 (July-Sept. 1938), pp. 438-64.

La Roncière, Charles de
"La France arctique ou les baleiniers basques au Spitzberg." Revue du Béarn et du Pays basque (1905), pp. 49-97.

Larousse, Pierre
Grand dictionnaire universel. Grand dictionnaire universel, Paris, 1905.

Laverdière, C.H.
Oeuvres de Champlain. Université Laval, Quebec City, 1870.

Lawrence, Mary
The Captain's Best Mate; The Journal of Mary Lawrence on the Whaler Addison, 1856-1860. Brown University Press, Providence, 1966.

Le Blant, Robert
"Une sédition basque à Terre-Neuve en 1690." Revue historique et archéologique du Béarn et du Pays basque (Jan.-Feb. 1932), pp. 46-64.

Le Moine, J.M.
Les pêcheries du Canada. Atelier typographique du Canadien, Quebec, 1863.

Le Roy de Bacqueville de la Potherie, Claude-Charles
Histoire de l'Amérique septentrionale. Jean-Luc Nion, Paris, 1722.

Leslie, John
Narrative of Discovery and Adventure in the Polar Seas and Regions: with Illustrations of their Climate, Geology, and Natural History; and an Account of the Whale-fishery. Oliver & Boyd, Edinburgh, 1835.

Lubbock, Basil
The Arctic Whalers. Brown, Son & Ferguson, Glasgow, 1937.

Macy, Obed
The History of Nantuckett. Hillard Gray, Boston, 1835.

Manby, George William
Journal of a Voyage to Greenland in the Year 1821. G. and W.B. Whitaker, London, 1823.

Markham, Albert Hastings
A Whaling-cruise to Baffin's Bay and the Gulf of Boothia and an Account of the Rescue of the Crew of the Polaris. S. Low, London, 1874.

Markham, Clement
"On the Whale-Fisheries of the Basque Provinces of Spain." Nature, Vol. 25 (1882), pp. 365-68.
---. Voyages of William Baffin, 1612-1622, Hakluyt Society, London, 1881.

Matthews, Leonard Harrison
A Note on Whaling. Clarendon Press, Oxford, 1968.
---. The Whale. Allen & Unwin, London, 1968.

McDougall, David J.
"The Shipbuilders, Whalers and Master Mariners of Gaspé Bay in the Nineteenth Century." In The Enterprising Canadians: Entrepreneurs and Economic Development in Eastern Canada, 1820-1914, L.R. Fischer and E.W. Sager, eds., Maritime History Group, St. John's, Nfld., 1979, pp. 123-145.

McFarland, Raymond
History of New England Fisheries. University of Pennsylvania, Philadelphia, 1911.

McLaughlin,W.R.D.
Call to the South. White Lion Pub., London, 1962.

McNab, Robert
The Old Whaling Days. Whitcombe and Tombs, Christchurch, 1913.

Melville, Herman
Moby Dick, or, The Whale. The Franklin Library, Franklin Centre, 1974.

Michel, Francisque
Le Pays basque. Firmin Diderot, Paris, 1857.

Millett, Samuel
A Whaling Voyage in the Bark Willis, 1849-1850. Published by the author, Boston, 1924.

Mitchell, Edward D.
"Les baleines dans le monde." Nature Canada, Vol. 2, No. 4 (Oct.-Dec. 1973).
---. Porpoise, Dolphin and Small Whale Fisheries of the World; Status and Problems. International Union for Conservation of Nature and Natural Resources, Morges, 1975.

Morel, M.F.
Bayonne, vues historiques et descriptives. Lamaignère, Bayonne, 1836.

Morley, F.V., and J.S. Hodgson
Whaling North and South. Methuen, London, 1927.

Moussette, Marcel
"La pêche à la baleine; méthodes de capture de la baleine utilisées dans le golfe et l'estuaire du Saint-Laurent." Revue d'histoire de la Gaspésie, Vol. 10, No. 1 (Jan.-Mar. 1972), pp. 16-30.

Mowat, Farley
A Whale for the Killing. McClelland & Stewart, Toronto, 1976.

Murdoch, W.G.B.
From Edinburgh to the Antarctic. Longmans, London, 1894.
---. Modern Whaling and Bear Hunting. Seeley Service, London, 1917.

Murphy, Robert Cushman
"The Way of the Sperm Whalers." Sea-Power, Vols. 2-3 (1917).

Musset, Lucien
"Quelques notes sur les baleiniers normands du Xe au XIIIe siècle." Revue d'histoire économique et sociale, Vol. 42, No. 2 (1964).

Narborough, John
An Account of Several Late Voyages and Discoveries to the South and North Towards the Streights of Magellan, the South Seas, the Vast Tracts of Land Beyond Hollandia Nova, also Towards Nova Zembla, Greenland or Spitsberg, Groynland or Engrondland. Sam Smith, London, 1694.

Noël, S.B.J.
Histoire générale des pêches anciennes et modernes. Imprimerie Royale, Paris, 1815.
---. Tableau historique de la pêche de la baleine. Fuchs, Paris, Year VIII of the Republic.

Nogaret, Joseph
"Petite histoire du Pays basque français." Bulletin de la Société des

sciences, lettres, arts et d'études régionales de Bayonne, Vol. 44, Nos. 1-2 (1923), pp. 1-96.

Nordhoff, C.
Whaling and Fishing. Dodd Mead, New York, 1895.

Norris, Kenneth S.
Whales, Dolphins and Porpoises. University of California Press, Los Angeles, 1966.

Olmstead, Francis Allyn
Incidents of a Whaling Voyage. D. Appleton, New York, 1841.

Patursson, Svere
"Whale Hunting in the Faroes." The Trident, Vol. 8, No. 90 (1946), p. 426.

Pedersen, Torbjorn
A Bibliography of Whales and Whaling. Jacob Dybwad, Oslo, 1946.

Peterson, Randolph L.
The Mammals of Eastern Canada. University of Toronto Press, Toronto, 1966.

Purchas, S.
Hakluytus Posthumus, or, Purchas His Pilgrimes. Hakluyt Society, Glasgow, 1906.

Rabot, Charles
"The Whale Fisheries of the World." Annual Report of the Smithsonian Institution (1913), pp. 481-89.

Rainey, Froelich G.
"The Whale Hunters of Tigara." Anthropological Papers of the American Museum of Natural History, Vol. 41, Part. 2 (1947), pp. 231-83.

Redgrave
"Journal of a Whaling Voyage from Dundee to Davis Straits, 1894." The Polar Record, Vol. 10, No. 65 (May 1960), pp. 126-35.

Reinfeld, Fred
Whales and Whaling. Garden City, New York, 1960.

Révoil, B. Henry
Pêches dans l'Amérique du Nord. Hachette, Paris, 1863.

Riedman, S.R., and E.T. Gustafson
Home is the Sea: For Whales. Rand McNally, Chicago, 1966.

Ritter, Raymond
"Victoire de quatre capitaines basques sur les baleiniers hollandais."

Bulletin de la Société des sciences, arts et lettres de Bayonne, No. 130 (1974).

Robertson, R.B.
Of Whales and Men. Alfred A. Knopf, New York, 1954.

Rochemonteix, Camille
Relation par lettres de l'Amérique septentrionale. Letouzey et Ané, Paris, 1904.

Rondelet, Guillaume
Histoire entière des poissons. M. Bonhomme, Lyon, 1558.

Ross, W. Gillies
Whaling and Eskimos: Hudson Bay, 1860-1915. National Museums of Canada, Ottawa, 1975.

Roy, Pierre-Georges
Les petites choses de notre histoire. 2nd ser., 2nd ed. Lévis, 1919.

Ruspoli, Mario
À la recherche du cachalot. Éditions de Paris, Paris, 1955.

Sanderson, Ivan T.
Follow the Whale. Little Brown, Boston, 1956.

Savary des Bruslons, Jacques
Dictionnaire universel de commerce, d'histoire naturelle et des arts et métiers. Philibert, Copenhagen, 1759. 5 vols.

Scammon, Charles M.
The Marine Mammals of the Northwestern Coast of North America Described and Illustrated, Together with an Account of the American Whale-fishery. Dover Publications, New York, 1968.

Scoresby, Jackson R.E.
The Life of William Scoresby. T. Nelson and Sons, London, 1861.

Scoresby, William
An Account of the Arctic Regions with a History and Description of the Northern Whale-fishery. Archibald Constable, Edinburgh, 1820. 2 vols.
---. The Arctic Regions and the Northern Whale-fishery. The Religious Tract Society, London, [1824].

Sergeant, David E.
"Whaling in Newfoundland and Labrador Waters." Norsk Hvalfangst-Tidende, Vol. 42, No. 12 (Dec. 1953), pp. 687-95.

Shapiro, Irwin
Story of Yankee Whaling. American Heritage, New York, 1959.

Slijper, E.J.
Whales. Hutchinson, London, 1962.

Smith, Charles Edward
From the Deep of the Sea: The Diary of Charles Edward Smith, Surgeon of the Whaleship Diana of Hull. P. Harris, Edinburgh, 1977.

Snelling, William Joseph
The Polar Regions of the Western Continent Explored. W.W. Reed, Boston, 1831.

Solyanik, A.
Cruising in the Atlantic; An Account of the Seventh Cruise of the Slava Whaling Flotilla. Foreign Languages Publication House, Moscow, 1956.

Southwell, Thomas
"Notes on the Seal and Whale-fishery of 1881." Natural History Society of Glasgow, Vol. 5 (Feb. 1882), pp. 215-21.

Spears, John R.
The Story of the New England Whalers. New York, Macmillan, 1908.

Stackpole, Edouard A.
The Sea-Hunters: The New England Whalemen during Two Centuries, 1635-1835. J.B. Lippincott, New York, 1953.
---. Whales and Destiny: The Rivalry Between America, France, and Britain for Control of the Southern Whale Fishery, 1785-1825. University of Massachusetts Press, [Boston], 1972.

Starbuck, Alexander
History of the American Whale-fishery from its Earliest Inception to the Year 1876. Argosy-Antiquarian, New York, 1964.

Tanner, V.
Outlines of the Geography, Life and Customs of Newfoundland-Labrador. O.Y. Tilgmann A.B., Helsinki, 1944.

Tower, Walter S.
"A History of the American Whale-fishery." Political Economy and Public Law, No. 20 (1907).

Uncle Philip
Uncle Philip's Conversations about the Whale Fishery and Polar Regions. Tegg & Son, London, 1837.

United States. Bureau of Fisheries.
A History of Whaling, with a Résumé of the Whaling Industry of the United States, 1937-1940. Government Printing Office, Washington, 1941.

Van Beneden, P.J.
"Un mot sur la pêche de la baleine et les premières expéditions arctiques." Académie royale de Belgique, 2nd ser., Vol. 46 (1878), pp. 967-85.

Venables, B.
Baleia, the Whalers of the Azores. The Bodley Head, London, 1968.

Verrill, A. Hyatt
The Real Story of the Whaler. D. Appleton, New York, 1916.

Veyrin, P.
Les Basques. 2nd ed. Bayonne, 1943.

Villiers, Alan J.
Whalers of the Midnight Sun; A Story of Modern Whaling in the Antarctic. Scribners, New York, 1944.
---. Whaling in the Frozen South. Bobbs-Merrill, Indianapolis, 1925.

Waterman, T.T.
The Whaling Equipment of the Makah Indians. University of Washington Press, Seattle, 1967.

Waymouth, George
"A True Relation of the Most Prosperous Voyage Made this Present Year, 1605, by Captain George Waymouth in the Discovery of the Land of Virginia, Where he Discovered, Sixty Miles up, a Most Excellent River; Together with a Most Fertile Land." Collections of the Massachusetts Historical Society, 3rd ser., Vol. 8 (1843), pp. 125-62.

White, Adam, ed.
A Collection of Documents on Spitsbergen and Greenland. New York, Burt Franklin, 1955.

Wilkes, Charles
Narrative of the United States Exploring Expedition During the Years 1838-1842. Lea & Blanchard, Philadelphia, 1845.

Yturbide, Pierre
"La pêche des baleines au Pays basque du XIIe au XVIIIe siècles." Société bayonnaise d'études régionales, Bull. Sup. No. 5 (1918).